The World Book of Children's Games

Arnold Arnold writes a widely syndicated education feature that has appeared in more than one hundred newspapers in the United States, Canada and Great Britain. He is also a designer with an international reputation, specializing in the development of play and learning materials. Many of these were the subject of a one-man exhibition at New York's Museum of Modern Art, and were featured in the *20th Century Design, USA* exhibition shown in major museums throughout America. Mr Arnold taught at and directed the Workshop School in New York where he introduced innovative teaching and learning methods. He is a Fellow of Boston University and the author of numerous books, including: *Art and Crafts for Children and Young People, Children's Games, Teaching and Learning from Birth to School Age, Violence and Your Child* and *Pictures and Stories from Forgotten Children's Books before 1850*, among others. His wife, whose professional name is Gail E. Haley, is a noted children's book author and illustrator, published in the United States, Great Britain and Japan. They and their two young children, Geoffrey and Marguerite, live in London.

**Also in the
Pan Child Development Series**

Your Child's Play
Arnold Arnold

Your Child's Health
Mary Manning

Problems of Childhood
Martin Herbert

The Child in the Family
Maria Montessori

Between Parent and Child
Haim G. Ginott

Your Baby Can Swim
Bonnie Prudden

Teach Your Baby to Read
Glenn Doman

Reading and Writing Before School
Felicity Hughes
with an introduction by Glenn Doman

Child Development Series

The World Book of Children's Games

Arnold Arnold

Pan Books in association with **Macmillan London**

First British edition published 1975 by Macmillan London Ltd
This edition published 1976 by Pan Books Ltd,
Cavaye Place, London SW10 9PG,
in association with Macmillan London Ltd
© Arnold Arnold 1972, 1975
ISBN 0 330 24814 6
Printed and bound in Great Britain by
Richard Clay (The Chaucer Press) Ltd, Bungay, Suffolk

Contents

Foreword 7

Introduction 13

The role of the parent or play supervisor, The rules of games, Winning and losing, Counting out, Choosing team captains and sides, Cheating, Organizing the game, Special suggestions for preschool children's games, Age grouping, Regulation games, How to use the age, place, and materials chart of games

1 Ball, bowling, beanbag, and balloon games 29
2 Marble games 72
3 Button games 86
4 Hop, skip, and jump 93
5 Race, tag, and catch games 106
6 Word games 138
7 Number games 175
8 Party games 187
9 Strategic games 210

Age, place, and materials chart of games 265
Bibliography 276
Picture sources 278
Index 281

To Gail, Francis, Marguerite
and Geoffrey;
to Buster, to the chipmunks,
to the ducks and to the turtles;
to the trees, to the grass,
to the wind on the water;
to the sun, to mud puddles and
to the lines on concrete pavements;
and to all the people and things
that awaken me to playfulness.

Foreword

American childhood traditions are inherited from abroad. Hence the original research for this book drew largely on British, European, African and Asian sources. It required little revision for publication in England.

There is as obvious a need for this book in Britain as in America. The United States, in addition to all its other troubles, has just ended a decade of educational ferment and confusion. Throughout the nineteen sixties American government supported a small army of academicians in order to discover behaviourist and technological alternatives to a humanistic education. These efforts did not succeed. Despite millions of dollars spent on educational research and supposed new methods of child care and rearing, hardly any were devoted to supporting and keeping alive the play lore and culture of childhood. Play and game traditions are not accidental. They are developmental neccessities. Crowding and lack of space, urbanization, TV addiction, and an obsession with pumping information into children have robbed many of playfulness and essential play experiences. Similar trends are now becoming apparent in Britain.

Apart from the exuberance producing, energy consuming, and whimsical aspects of game playing, it is crucial for socializing and educating children. It aids the formation of conscience and ethical concepts. It dramatizes the need for rules. Today's family, school and community fail children in these respects in Britain as in America. The decline in space and opportunities for play coincide with a rise in juvenile delinquency. This increase in unruliness is attributable in some measure to a discontinuity of child culture caused by a hostile, post-industrial environment.

Jean Piaget, the noted Swiss psychologist, has investigated the role and the importance of game playing in young children. *'For the young child, a rule is a sacred reality because it is traditional; for the older ones it depends on mutual agreement . . . The game of marbles, for instance, as played by boys, contains an extremely complex system of rules, that is to say, a code of laws, a jurisprudence of its own . . . All morality consists of a system of rules, and the essence of all morality is to be sought for in the respect which the individual acquires for these rules . . . The little boys who are beginning to play are gradually trained by the older ones in respect for the law. As to the older ones, it is in their power to alter the rules. If this is not "morality", then where does morality begin?'*

The quality of unruliness among some of today's young people suggests a form of arrested development concerning their abilities to formulate viable ethical judgments. This could be due to a relative lack of game playing in their younger days if, as Piaget suggests, formation of conscience depends in large measure on such experience. One example suffices to dramatize the misunderstanding of the function of rules among university students. It is representative of many youth attitudes during the nineteen sixties, some of which prevail today.

Two Massachusetts Institute of Technology graduate students visited me in New York to show me a game one of them had invented. It had, according to them, won the approval and admiration of their professors. If true, this was a sad comment on the quality of their instructors. The game

* Piaget, Jean, et al., *The Moral Judgment of the Child,* London: Routledge, Kegan & Paul.

was explained as the first totally non-aggressive game played without any rules whatsoever. The students were somewhat taken aback when I pointed out that this seemed to me to be the first 'rule' of their 'no-rule' game. Undaunted, they explained that anyone could begin and play when and how he liked, moving playing pieces across the game board at random. Winning and losing was determined entirely by how each player 'felt' at the end of the game. These, of course, were further rules, though the inventor failed to appreciate this fact. Nonetheless I wagered that I could 'win' and make them 'lose' positively at the end of the game.

After they completed their random moves at random turns I stacked the playing pieces, folded the game board and stuck the lot into my pocket. They were rather offended. Just as they had not recognized the rules implicit in their pretended anarchy, so had they failed to discern the obvious winning strategy. This incident would have been very funny, were it not typical of the misjudgments, the misbehaviour, the inability to foresee consequences, that stem from such absurd premises. It is representative of large portions of the child and youth population that, since World War II, have ruled themselves out of the game due to their lack of play experience.

These same attitudes are echoed in Britain's football hooliganism of today. It should not be confused with the game-inspired violence, common during the reign of James I, cited in chapter II. There is a considerable difference between the aggressive behaviour of players and that inspired among spectators. Games are aggressive by definition. In animals instinct provides essential limitations to aggressiveness between members of the same species. They are released from such inhibitions only in times of extreme stress and ecological disaster. In human beings aggressiveness is governed by rules and by a supposed capacity to weigh the consequences of breaking them. Games symbolize and demonstrate the need for rules in real life.

Children who play games can develop non-violent, though aggressively playful attitudes. They learn that a game can only be played successfully according to rules to which all players subscribe voluntarily. But those condemned by circumstances to remain perpetual spectators, either at home before the TV set or in the grandstands, tend to confuse team cooperation with violent bravado. They misinterpret the players' aggressiveness.

In Britain, now also overwhelmed by the heritage of mindless industrialization and urbanization, child culture is threatened as in America. England's children have become less active and playful, and more restricted and TV addicted than those of the past. There is constant attrition of open play spaces. Conscientious parents and teachers in Britain are increasingly concerned over how, where, and when to give children opportunities for active and creative play. If Britain's past battles were first acted out on the playing fields of Eton, its current struggles are viewed passively by children trapped before the telly inside their homes in a prevailing and increasingly poisonous urban environment.

Informal game playing is no cure-all. But it offers parents, teachers, recreation, youth and therapy workers opportunities to help make up some of the social and cultural deficits suffered by most contemporary children. In addition to having childhood traditions kept alive for them, children need ample opportunities and space for social, informal play at home, in schools, and in the community. Traffic and crowding rob many of the freedom to romp, explore and play on their own. Neither lip service to 'de-schooling' nor a return to authoritarianism can make up for these lacks.

Children in today's society don't need less, but better, kinder, and more informed supervision. Ultimately they will need entirely different communities than those we now provide, before they can rediscover and pass the culture of childhood from one generation to the next by word of mouth, without adult supervision. Children will be able to maintain their play lore unaided only when we have survived this age of cultural discontinuity and social isolation. I hope that this book will serve as a repository of the now interrupted game culture of childhood until that healthier day.

Arnold Arnold
London 1975

Introduction

This book addresses itself to parents, to teachers, to recreational, park, playground, and street supervisors of children's play, and to children. It includes selected indoor and outdoor games, other than formal sports, for children from preschool to primary school ages. Older children and teenagers can similarly enjoy some of these. I have made the selection and adapted the rules with a consideration of today's child life at home, in the school, and in the community.

There is a special need for this book at this time. Family life and childhood traditions are now threatened with destruction in an environment that is essentially hostile to child development. Crowded cities, suburbs, and schools; the lack of safe play spaces and fresh air; and TV addiction conspire to destroy the spirit of spontaneous play and the culture of childhood.

In her introduction to Alice Gomme's *The Traditional Games of England, Scotland and Ireland*, the folklorist Dorothy Howard expresses the hope that with republication of this classic, 'children's folk lore is climbing the ladder of academic and scholarly respectability on this side of the ocean.' But at the same time she deplores 'appropriating old games and revamping them to fit supervised play programmes ... to transmit by book the old games and play ways which children have transmitted to children on playgrounds for hundreds of years.'[21]

It is obviously preferable when children can perpetuate this culture from generation to generation by word of mouth. But Miss Howard, like so many others, seems strangely unsympathetic to the restrictions placed on today's children by a hazardous society that inhibits their humanizing development and the spontaneous perpetuation of play culture. And so I have attempted to rescue a portion of this lore that is applicable by today's child from being abandoned entirely to the folklorist, to the cultural anthropologist, and to 'academic respectability.' It must remain the property of children, even when it needs to be kept alive for them by adults.

A definition of game-playing is difficult because it overlaps in some areas with play with toys. Much of children's play with toys is exploratory; some involves *role-playing*. But all game-playing involves acting. A game can therefore be roughly classified as an activity in which the child assumes a particular role, as aggressor or defender, and characteristics of models outside himself. The common ground in play as in games is, in the words of the historian Johan Huizinga, 'doing a thing for the sake of the thing itself.'[23]

I have left out a number of game categories quite deliberately. Some seemed inappropriate to wide application by today's children. Others are so specialized that they should be, as some are, the subject of books of their own. Games with tops, games involving songs and stories, and string and finger games like Cat's Cradle are excluded, although I refer to them in the text and in the bibliography.[19, 22]

Each game in this book is prefaced with information that

suggests the lowest age group to which it might be introduced. I am generally opposed to any age-grouping of activities, books, records, or toys, since each child differs from the next in development and in experience. But these games are predominantly group games, and so some average age-grouping seemed advisable. Games should be introduced to younger age groups on a trial basis. They must be halted or modified when children demonstrate their lack of enjoyment or their immaturity by being unable to cooperate, or when losing still overwhelms them.

Most of today's adults no longer know the large repertoire of childhood games with which previous generations were familiar. Spontaneous play opportunities were already restricted in their childhood. Our young parents and teachers are the first generation to have spent a large part of their growing years in front of TV sets. They therefore have little play and game information that they can transmit to their children. Teenagers, even when younger children have contact with them, suffer an even greater lack of informal game experience.

Until the beginning of this century the more mature children in the family predominantly cared for the younger ones. Preschool children could observe their older brothers and sisters at play in fields, in gardens, in playgrounds, and in relatively safe residential streets. Two hundred years ago, the games of children past infancy were identical to those played by adults on village greens in the summer and before the hearth in winter. Children needed only to imitate what they saw their elders do all around them.

The industrial revolution first interrupted this general playfulness. The eighteenth-century German educator Friedrich Froebel recognized that such a lack of models might inhibit children's learning and maturation. He suggested a system of education involving games – 'mother play' – that he hoped might serve as a substitute for spontaneous childhood culture. But it was soon turned into a regimen of formal learning by the schoolmasters and parents of that day.

Lately, play has been rediscovered as a learning instrument. But now it threatens to turn into yet another form of child manipulation, of teaching the child 'cognitive' information, while neglecting the socializing and experiential aspects of play.

Before a child can benefit from formal education, he needs development of self-expression, inner controls, coordination, and the faculties of whimsy, humour, curiosity, and foresight.[2] He must experience leadership and learn to appreciate the need for submitting to rules. He must be allowed to succeed and to learn how to accept failure gracefully. He needs the enjoyment of active participation in rewarding activities and of total absorption. Games can help a child acquire some of these qualities and skills. Informal games allow every child, regardless of his talents or weaknesses, to participate as an equal with other children and to enjoy experiences that are essential to his future learning.

Many of today's school sports are organized so as to exclude all but the most able performers. The rest of the student body watches from the sidelines, a habit that is reinforced at home in front of the TV set. As a result, many are denied physical exercise and a foundation for social and academic learning. At the same time our children are severely restricted at home and in school, despite the lip service given to their emancipation. Adults vacillate from permissiveness to authoritarianism Neither treatment allows children the exercise of making choices or of formulating rules for themselves in trial situations. Only a child who has these experiences early and often in play can learn to make distinctions between what is playful and what is merely ludicrous, or between aggressive pursuit of goals and antagonism.

As repeatedly stressed in the following chapters, children should be encouraged to make up and to agree to rules of their

own invention, rather than merely to follow those that are given. Only then can they learn the fundamental rule that no game, nor any aspect of life, can be enjoyed without rules.

The 'no-rule' idea that is central to many of today's youth attitudes is the product of their relative inexperience in social play. Today's child never has sufficient experience in play to realize that 'no rules allowed' is in itself a rule. In order to play 'the no-rule game' a whole raft of new rules naturally follow, whether or not anarchic players admit to them.[4]

I have included historic sidelights concerning the origins of some of the games I have adapted. Telling children about their history can help them establish a bond with the past. It will give them incentives for carrying this heritage forward into the future.

The following notes and comments are especially addressed to those who organize or supervise children's games at home or in school.

The role of the play supervisor
An experienced teacher usually knows how much direction and supervision is required to organize groups of children. But despite this knowledge and the best of intentions, many

manage to turn game-playing in class or in the playground into a form of discipline or even punishment. The role of the game supervisor should be restricted to suggesting and initiating play, helping children acquire the required skills, furnishing materials, and acting as arbiter when they are unable to manage on their own.

Preschool children need a great deal of help when they first play group games. They cannot be *made* to play. Regimentation will certainly kill their enthusiasm and their ability to learn how to handle the materials of play, how to follow rules, and how to take their turn. Older children should be encouraged to adapt given rules and to make up others, to improvise, and to regulate themselves and each other. They must be given opportunities to operate within their group as leaders and as followers. The presence of a respected and unobtrusive adult or teenager can serve as a regulating influence on school-age children's play.

The rules of games

Except in formal sports, like cricket, netball or football, that are governed by standard regulations, and when children are not especially sports-minded, it is best to encourage them to formulate rule variations by agreement among themselves. Stimulate group discussions beforehand on how the game is to be played. But insist on elimination of any rule that discriminates against unpopular, smaller, or weaker players, or that might lead to inflicting pain or causing damage.

Some play supervisors feel that a major lesson of game-playing for children is their submission to ordained rules. But in many instances, this merely leads to resistance or to passivity. Children can only recognize the value of rules and respect those that apply to games and to life in general if they are given opportunities for inventing rules and for trying them out.

Winning and losing

It is important to realize that children below the age of 5 or 6 find it extremely difficult to accept the idea of losing. Organize game variations that involve neither winning nor losing. In game-playing by children of any age greatest emphasis should be placed on exuberance and on the fun of playing. Children, especially today, are sufficiently competitive without being driven to succeed even in their informal games. The very nature of games is competitive. Nothing is wrong with providing outlets for beneficial aggressive behaviour. But considerable damage can result from making winning seem the sole value, more important than any others that are implicit in game-playing. So in most instances, do not reward the child or team who wins and do not condone forfeits or punishment of losers. Victory in a game won through skill and competence should be a sufficient reward. Losing should not lead to a sense of defeat. Instead, it can stimulate greater effort, or better coordination, or more concentration, or finer cooperation on the next occasion.

The play supervisor should suggest group games for young children in which each can experience accomplishment. And

at a party, such as a birthday party, the adult in charge should arrange things so that each child wins something, if prizes are to be given. The idea is to make all the children happy, rather than to pit one against the next.

For these reasons among others, a number of variations are suggested for many of the games listed. Some require a losing member of a team to be 'out' of the game when he fails or is tagged. Alternative rules allow such an 'out' player to join the opposing side, the last remaining player of his original team being the winner. Other possibilities are to keep each team's turn 'at bat' to a short period of time. Then the 'out' players re-enter the game without a long wait. Still another option is the starting of a smaller side game for those who are eliminated from the larger one for the time being. Allowing a number of players to stand around aimlessly while the rest are playing can lead to unhappiness.

The informed play supervisor should address himself to issues such as these instead of becoming deeply involved in the game itself. If the game palls and interest lags, the super-

visor should suggest another activity. This book contains dozens of possible games for every age group, and in using them the children may invent variations of their own. The leader should never insist on completing a given number of rounds of the same game before allowing a change of activity. This is how children lose interest in games and why they feel regimented by adults.

Counting out, choosing team captains and sides
The tendency among many who organize and supervise games is to choose team captains or to allow each team to elect its own. In the first instance children suspect favouritism, whether or not they are justified. In the second, teams may choose a leader merely because he is the most powerful member of that group. He may intimidate or bully the rest.

More important than fostering leadership in favoured or in seemingly dominant children is to give every child a chance to experience authority and responsibility. Assign an order of play in which every player is a leader in turn. This is preferable to leaving the choice to children, to chance, or to counting out, in which adroit youngsters can always manipulate the odds.

The following are some of the favourite methods of selecting a player to be 'it,' choosing leaders, or deciding the order of play that children usually use when they play without supervision.

1 Tossing a coin. Players are required to guess 'heads' or 'tails' of a coin flipped by one player. The first player to guess correctly is 'it' or the first to play, and so on. Team selections can be made by all children flipping coins, the 'heads' joining one team and the 'tails' the other. If the game requires equal-sized teams, coin-tossing continues among the larger team, until both are evened out.

2 Drawing straws. The game organizer, or one of the players, holds a number of straws (or blades of grass, ribbons, or strings) in his hand. All but one are the same length. He holds them so that the rest of the players cannot tell which is the odd-sized one. Each player chooses one straw. That player who picks the odd-sized one is 'it,' goes first, or becomes leader of one of the teams. To choose teams, the game organizer selects an equal number of short and long straws and holds them out as before. Players are divided according to which size straw they pick.

3 Odds or evens. The game organizer, or one of the players or team captains, holds out a number of fingers on both hands, behind his back, out of sight of the rest of the players. Each of the other players in turn then guesses whether the number of stretched-out fingers is odd or even, to decide teams, order of play, and so on. The game organizer can let each player see the number of his outstretched fingers after he has made his guess, and may then change the number for the next player.

4 Racket toss-up. In games requiring a racket, the choice of first turn, team membership, or leadership of teams can be decided by flipping the racket and letting one side or the other determine the results, according to the side facing up at each toss.

5 Hand-over-hand. In games requiring a bat (like rounders), captains and order of play may be decided by one player tossing the bat to the next, who must catch it. The first player then grasps the bat directly above the hand of the second, who in turn grasps the next higher position with his other hand, and so on. The player whose hand comes closest to the top of the bat, still grasping it, but not placing any part of his hand beyond it, wins that decision, or joins a particular team.

6 Playing-card choice. If available, a pack of ordinary playing cards, one dealt to each player, may decide team captain, sides, or order of play. After one card has been dealt to each player, the player holding the highest card goes first, or becomes team captain, and so on. Sides can be chosen by putting those holding red cards on one team and those holding black cards on the other.

7 Counting rhymes. Nursery and other special rhymes have been used from time immemorial to count out sides, to determine playing order, and to choose team leaders. One player recites the verse while the rest stand around in a circle. The reciting player points his finger at any player, chosen supposedly at random, and moves that finger from player to player on each succeeding word – (or it might be done on syllables or letters). The player to whom his finger is pointing at the last word of the counting rhyme is 'it,' the team leader, or the member of one team. For choosing sides, the counting out continues until the first team, equal in number to the remainder, is chosen. Any experienced child can cheat easily in counting out. He can choose on whom the last syllable falls, knowing with which player to start, or, as often happens, by skipping a child as he recites and points.[20] Following are a few old and common counting rhymes:

Eena, mena, mina, mo,
Catch an outlaw by the toe;
If he hollers, let him go,
Eena, mena, mina, mo!

Intery, mintery, cutery, corn,
Apple-seed and briar-thorn,
Wire, briar, limber lock,
Three geese in a flock;
One flew east, one flew west,
One flew over the cuckoo's nest
O-U-T, out!

Apples and oranges, two for a penny,
Takes a good scholar to count as many;
O-U-T, out goes she [or he].

Monkey, monkey, bottle of beer,
How many monkeys are there here?
1, 2, 3,
You are he [or she].

As I went up the apple-tree,
All the apples fell on me;
Bake a pudding, bake a pie,
Did you ever tell a lie?
Yes you did; you know you did,
You broke your mother's teapot lid.
L-I-D, that spells, lid.

Cheating
Cheating in games is more often a time-honoured custom than
a frowned-on practice in many adult societies. The unpardon-
able crime, in most cultures that accept cheating, is being
caught in the act. But it is considered the height of cleverness
to get away with it unnoticed. We also accept this practice in
real life, though we insist on entirely different standards of
behaviour from our children, who naturally resent it.

It is far better to dramatize the socially disruptive effect of
cheating than to moralize about it to children. Games are an
ideal vehicle to teach this lesson. This concept is implied in
the ritual and customs of those societies that realistically
accept cheating as allowable behaviour in real life as in games,
subject to given rules. The shaming of those who are caught
in the act serves better to inhibit cheating than a blanket prohibition.

For these reasons I suggest that you invite players, old
enough to appreciate this idea, to cheat at games with the
understanding that they may suffer banishment from the game

if they are caught. Occasionally encourage a game in which all are invited to cheat without penalty. The game is bound to be sufficiently chaotic and unpleasant so that the players themselves will request an end to this rule.

Organizing the game

Whether parent, professional teacher, or teenager, the game supervisor has a number of clearly defined responsibilities:

1 Become familiar with the requirements and rules for each game to be played. Furnish all the necessary equipment and materials before the game begins.

2 Have an understanding of children, their talents, abilities and disabilities.

3 Suggest only games that are within the competence of the age groups involved, and that are appropriate to their size, strength, and experience. Steer children away from games that are too complicated or too difficult at their stage of development.

4 Avoid over-enthusiasm. Children rapidly spot and distrust fake enthusiasm and artificial cheer.

5 Be prepared to participate as a regular player, subject to all rules, including those that may seem to detract from adult dignity, if you are needed to even up teams. Otherwise watch from the side lines.

6 Help children who may not be as competent and well-coordinated as their age mates by assigning them jobs or positions that allow them the exercise of whatever skills they possess. A handicapped child may enjoy being timekeeper, scorer, or referee in a game in which he himself cannot participate. Overlook mistakes of individual children, or quietly correct them without interrupting the game. Don't embarrass children or scold them in front of the others for an inadvertent infraction of rules, or error in play.

7 Explain one game at a time, and let the children play one or more trial games that don't 'count' before the actual game begins. Have a number of alternative games and the required equipment available in advance, in case the children do not like the first game you suggested.

8 Let the children rest between games, as their ages and energy dictate.

9 Select games in a chronology of difficulty, starting with the simplest, and working up to more challenging ones as the children's skills improve through practice.

Special suggestions for preschool children's games
Preschool children cannot follow complicated rules. Choose games for young age groups that develop individual skills, like ball-throwing or hitting a target with a beanbag, rather than competitive team games. Gather preschool children around you as you explain what is expected and give demonstrations of what is to be done. Pick out one or two able children and allow them to demonstrate what you showed them. Then gradually involve more and more of the rest, until all or most of them are in the game. Have alternative activities ready for those who choose not to participate. Keep alert for the time

when the interest of the playing children seems to wane. Then suggest that they vary game-playing with another activity, unless the children themselves insist on playing longer.

Preschool and infant-school children find it difficult to await taking turns. Some feel discriminated against when they are 'it,' though they may have enjoyed playing while others were 'it.' It is best to keep such children out of team games, until they can observe game-playing long and often enough to submit willingly to the discipline required to play them. Never force a child to participate.

Plan the time-span of such games to be short, and keep groups or teams small, so that all have a turn before the majority tire of the game. It is better to play several short rounds than to insist on a single long one.

Age grouping
The games listed in this book state approximate age groups. But your knowledge and observation of the children are the best indicators of which games they are ready to play. Simplify the rules or change the game if it proves too difficult.

Regulation games

This book includes only games that can be played informally at home, in classrooms, in schoolyards or back gardens, playgrounds, parks and fields, or on beaches. Ample rule manuals for formal sports and regulation games exist for those who wish to learn to play them. The informal games listed in this book are a useful preparation for those that involve throwing, kicking, or other coordination. They have special appeal not only to young children, but also to older ones who are not especially athletic.

How to use the age, place, and materials chart of games

In each chapter throughout this book, games are grouped in an ascending order of complexity. To facilitate location of games that are appropriate for particular age groups, all but the Strategic Games are listed in the chart at the end of this book, showing category, number of given variations, age group, the minimum number of required players, needed equipment, and the place where they can be played – indoors, at home, in the classroom, or in the gym; outdoors, on the beach, in the grass, in a car, on a paved street or playground – and page number. All games are also listed by name in the Index.

The age grouping of these games furnishes rough guidelines only, as experience and such developmental differences as size, strength, coordination, and intelligence vary from child to child and from group to group.

The strategic games are listed in the chart only by name, by the number of required players, and by page number, in an order of family relationships. They can be played wherever a game diagram can be scratched into the ground, drawn on a pavement or on a piece of paper. These games are generally unsuitable for children below school age. Even older children need to play the more elementary games many times before they can develop the insight, planning ability, and logic required for the more difficult ones.

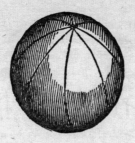

I
Ball, Bowling, Beanbag, and Balloon Games

The playing ball is probably the simplest and most readily available toy that lends itself to the greatest variety of games for a child alone or for children in groups. Any two or more children who meet for the first time, whether or not they speak the same language, will find an ordinary playing ball an immediate bridge to understanding.

The origins of ball games and sports go back many centuries. Most have evolved slowly through the ages. For example basketball, 'invented' in 1892 in Springfield, Massachusetts, by Dr. James Naismith, was really adapted from a Floridian Indian game. The ball, the solid sphere and the inflated skin, predates historical times.

The first ball was probably a stone or a pebble, thrown as much as a weapon as for tests of skill. Its use in play was most likely a preparation for hunting, defence, or attack. A smooth, rounded stone obviously felt better in the hand and could be thrown farther than a jagged one. When it landed it rolled, so it lent itself better to games of skill in which control, rather than sheer strength, determined success. Many thousands of

years must have gone by before man discovered that he himself could shape and polish stones, and so turn them into perfect spheres. A ball of this type which is more than 5,000 years old is exhibited in London's British Museum.

Only one or two isolated tribes exist anywhere in the world to whom the ball as a toy or as a weapon is unknown. Most civilizations have, at one time or another, attributed magical qualities to this shape and to games in which balls were used. One African society in the former French Cameroons still believes that during times of drought, girls can invoke rainfall through ritual ball-game playing.[6] In medieval times, choir boys played similar religious games.

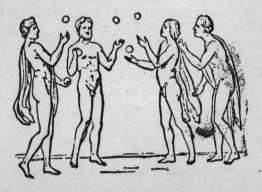

A mural in an ancient Egyptian tomb at Beni Hasan shows two girls tossing a ball back and forth. In his epic *Odyssey*, the Greek poet Homer tells of ball games at the time of the siege of Troy. During the period in which Alexander the Great ruled, Athenians erected a statue to that ruler's favourite ball-player. Julius Caesar and Emperor Augustus were eager ball-players, as was Harun al-Rashid of *A Thousand and One Nights* fame. The Celts of pre-Christian Ireland played ball as a part of their religious rites. Neighbouring villages contested for the possession of the sun, as represented by a ball made of an inflated goat-bladder. And the game of Handball is still a national sport in Ireland.

The citizens of European towns in the Middle Ages were so fond of ball games that they built special high-ceilinged arenas called 'ball houses.' Here they could play regardless of weather or season. The same halls were also used for singing and dancing contests. From this practice came the designations *ballad*, *ballet*, and *ball* – songs and dances that took their names from the places in which they were performed.

Today's spectators at football grounds and in front of TV sets may become noisily agitated or jubilant when their favourite teams lose or score. But their excitement is nothing compared to the enthusiasm or degree of spectator participation common at ball games in France in the seventeenth century. The game then popular was similar to football. It led to serious injuries, fractures, and sometimes worse fates to both players and fans. Whole towns and villages would battle with each other and at times feud for years over the outcome of games. Thus, in 1639, the French King Charles V banned all public games by royal decree. But they were so popular that even this prohibition had little effect.

Hurling, originally played by the Romans, and taken up by the British in the fifteenth century, gave birth to many of the rules of today's sports, such as football and rugger. In the English version, houses that were miles apart were designated as goals. Players ranged over the countryside, converging on the ball-carrier 'so as you shall sometimes see twenty or thirty lie tugging together in the water [of shallow streams and ditches] scrambling and scratching for the ball.'[32]

Camp was the name of a football game known in England as early as the fourteenth century and not very different from the Greek and Norse Common Ball, or Ball Battle, and other games in which players were often severely wounded and sometimes killed. The name of this game probably came from the medieval German word *Kemp*, which meant warrior or champion. There the game of *Kemping*, played until late in the nineteenth century, consisted of one team of men hurling wooden balls, loaded with lead, against another team. The interrelationship of these various games is illustrated by the fact that nineteenth-century schoolboys in Massachusetts spoke of 'camping' a ball, meaning to kick it.

The extremes of violence to which the games of five and six hundred years ago led in England caused them to be outlawed there as they were in France. King Edward III attempted to do so in 1349, giving as the excuse that ball-playing interfered with the practice of archery among the population. King James I tried again to forbid such games in the seventeenth century, declaring that 'From this court I debarre all rough and violent exercises, as the foot-ball, meeter for lameing than making able the users thereof.'[32]

Balls have in various times and places been made of papyrus, plaited rushes, stone, marble, wood, pottery, terra cotta, and animal hides or cloth filled with hay, kapok, shavings, sawdust, and seeds. American Indians in pre-Columbian times played with balls made of sewn deer hides. And Japanese children, on special holidays, are still given balls made of tightly wadded tissue paper wound round with coloured string. While the sap of the rubber tree was long used in South America and Africa for a variety of purposes, the invention of the solid bouncing ball had to await the discovery,

early in the nineteenth century, of the process of vulcanizing rubber. Though many of today's sports balls are still made of rubber or have a rubber core or bladder, plastics are replacing this material in the manufacture of most balls for children.

Histories of some ball games, played by individuals or in groups, in which the ball is thrown, kicked, headed, rolled, or struck with a stick, mallet, bat, or racket, are treated briefly in the rules to certain games included in this selection. But no matter how a ball is used in play, it is a most satisfactory toy. It is not surprising that we enjoy it so much. It is symbolic of the globe on which we live.

Pitch ball
Ages: 4 and older.
Number of players: 2 or more.
Equipment: 3 beanbags (or soft rubber balls, table tennis balls, or golf balls); chalk; wastepaper basket.
Place: Indoors (classroom or any other room or gym) or outdoors.

A starting line is marked with chalk, a stick, or a tape, six feet or more from the wastepaper basket. Players line up behind the chalk line, each one stepping up to it in turn. The first player receives three balls (or whatever other equipment is used) at each turn, and tries to pitch them into the wastepaper basket, one at a time. He scores according to the number he manages to toss inside. The next player, and each in turn, is given the three balls and plays as did the first. That player wins who gets the highest score. This game can be played for one or for several rounds.

Variation: Many different targets can be used, including several pots and pans, lined up side by side, each of which is assigned a different score value. A target can be made out of a corrugated box into the top of which several holes have been cut, each hole large enough for the pitched ball to pass through. Each hole can be given a different score value. Or, if beanbags are used, a three-concentric-ring target can be drawn on the floor, the centre ring marked 100, the second ring 50, and the outer ring 20. Players score either when their bag is tossed so that it is inside one of the target areas, without touching any of the drawn circles, or, when played by younger children, if the bag lands on one of the lines.

Bell ball

Ages: 5 and older.

Number of players: 1 or more.

Equipment: Medium-sized inflated ball (or hollow rubber ball, beanbag, or inflated balloon); a bell on a string, ribbon, or stick.

Place: Outdoors – the bell is hung on a limb or on the branch of a tree, or from any other projection, 6 feet above the ground. Indoors – only a beanbag or balloon should be used.

A line is marked off at a distance from the bell, from which each player throws, that will both challenge him and at the same time allow him a fair chance of hitting the bell with the ball, beanbag, or balloon. Each player may have a number of turns, agreed to before the start of the game. Each time a player hits the bell, he scores one point. The highest-scoring player wins.

Patsy ball

Ages: 6 and older.
Number of players: 1 or more.
Equipment: Small, bouncing rubber ball.
Place: Outdoors on hard ground or pavement.

Each player in turn pats the ball between bouncing it on the ground. He scores according to the number of times he pats the ball without allowing it to bounce more than once between pats. Whenever a player misses, the ball is passed to the next player, if any, and so on. That player wins who can keep the ball bouncing and pat it alternately the greatest number of times.

Variation: The player is allowed to pat the ball only with his left (or right) hand. Another method is for the player to pat the ball alternately with his left and right hands between bounces.

Sevens

Ages: 6 and up.
Number of players: 1 or more.
Equipment: Small, bouncing rubber ball.
Place: Outdoors or gym.

The object of this game is for each player to catch and throw the ball in 7 (or more or less) set ways without fumbling or dropping it. At any point at which the player fails to follow the agreed upon sequence, or drops the ball, he stops and surrenders the ball to the next player. He scores himself according to the number of catches and throws he completes successfully before dropping the ball or mixing up the sequence.

The name of this game and the reason for restricting the number of throws to seven are probably connected with the magic assigned to particular numbers in primitive religions. The number 7, in ancient myth, has been assumed to have magical qualities. This, like many other myths, has survived in children's play. So there is no reason why the number of sequences for each turn cannot be altered to more or less, according to the attention span and skill of players at different ages and stages of development.

Following are some sequences commonly used:

1 Throw the ball up against a wall and catch it 3 times.

2 Throw the ball up into the air 3 times, clapping your hands after each throw and before you catch it.

3 The same as (2) above, but clap your hands behind your back before you catch the ball.

4 The same as (2) above, but clap your hands, and then touch each shoulder with your opposite hand before you catch the ball.

5 Throw the ball up in the air 3 times with your left hand, catching it in your right hand each time it returns.

6 The same as (5) above, but reverse hands: throw with your right; catch with your left.

7 Throw the ball 3 times with one hand from behind your back, up over your head, and catch it with the other hand in front. Then repeat, using opposite hands for catching and throwing.

8 Bounce the ball on the ground 3 times, turn completely around, and catch it each time before it bounces again.

9 Bounce the ball on the ground with your right hand, and lift your leg over it before you catch it on the rebound. Do this 3 times with one hand and leg. Then do it 3 times using your other hand and leg.

10 Throw the ball into the air 3 times, reciting: 'Peter Piper picked a peck of pickled peppers' before catching it each time.

11 Throw the ball into the air. Let it bounce off your head before catching it.

12 Beat the ball down onto the ground 3 times in succession and then catch it . . . and so on.

Pass the ball
Ages: 6 and older.
Number of players: 6 or more.
Equipment: Medium-sized inflated ball.
Place: Outdoors with ball. Indoors with balloon.

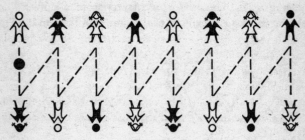

Players line up in two equal rows, facing one another, as far apart as they can throw and catch the ball. The first player, at the head of either line, throws the ball to that player directly opposite him, who returns it to the player in the opposite row, second in line from the first. Play continues until the last player has caught the ball. He then returns it, and play continues in the opposite direction, and so on, for a number of rounds determined before the start of the game.

Any player who drops the ball at his turn steps back one step (or shoe's length for very young or inexperienced players). After three such fumbles and backward steps, that player is out of the game.

When a player has stepped back, but manages to catch and return the ball without dropping it in the following two consecutive turns, he may step into line again, or one step forward, whichever is the lesser distance. That side wins which has the largest number of players remaining in line at the end of the game.

Variation 1: Players are divided into two equal teams, each of which forms a circle, each player standing 1·5 metres (5 feet) or more from the next. The players then throw the ball from one to the next around the circle. Each team plays with its own ball. All other rules of the original game remain as before.

Variation 2: Players are divided into two equal teams. Each team divides in half. Half the players on one team form a single line, standing alternately next to half the players on the opposing team. The remaining players form a similar line, each player facing a member of the opposing team in the first

line (see diagram). The opposing team members at one end of the two lines are given a ball each. Each throws the ball to his own next team member diagonally opposite him. When each ball reaches the last team member in line, play continues in the opposite direction. Play continues for as many rounds, from one end of each line to the other, as agreed upon before the beginning of the game. That team wins whose first player has the ball in hand at the end of the agreed-upon number of rounds.

Call ball
Ages: 6 and older.
Number of players: 5 or more.
Equipment: Small, soft, bouncing rubber ball.
Place: Outdoors or gym.

Each player is given a special name – in the case of 7 players, each becomes a 'day of the week.' One of the secondary benefits of a game like this one is that it can be used by a parent or teacher to reinforce memory. Children are much more likely to remember the days of the week or the months of the year used in play than by sitting in a classroom or at home, trying to memorize them by rote.

The first player 'up' bounces the ball off the ground or floor as hard as he can, calling out the name of any other player as he does so. All other players are loosely grouped around him. As soon as the ball leaves the first player's hand, all other players scatter. That player whose name is called must try to catch the ball before it bounces a second time. If he succeeds, he is next 'up,' and bounces the ball, as did the first player 'up.' If the player whose name was called fails to catch the ball in time, he loses one point and calls 'STOP.' All other players must stand wherever they are. The named player then aims the ball at any other player, except at that player who called his name. If another player is struck or tagged with the ball, he loses one point and is 'up' at that turn. If no player is tagged, then the player whose name was called by the first player loses another point, and the first player is 'up' once more. Any player who loses three points is out of the game. The last remaining player or players win the game.

Variation 1: If a windowless wall is available, the first 'up' player may bounce the ball at the wall, calling out any other player's name. That player must try to catch the ball after the first and before the second bounce on the ground. The rest of the rules stand.

Variation 2: A square, large enough to hold all players including the first 'up' player, is drawn on the ground or floor. All except the 'up' player may run out of the square as soon as the ball is thrown. They return for each 'up' turn. The rest of the rules remain the same.

Tag ball

Ages: 6 and older.   *Equipment:* Large inflated ball.
Number of players: 3 or more.   *Place:* Outdoors or gym.

One player is 'it,' and is given the ball, while the rest scatter.
'It' tries to tag any other player by throwing the ball. The
tagged player then changes places with 'it' and continues in
turn. A player may only be considered tagged if the ball hits
him before it bounces. Players may return the ball to 'it' to
speed up the game. All players may run, including 'it.'
Variation 1: A player may be considered 'tagged' if the ball
touches him even after it has bounced one or more times.
Variation 2: In a game of 12 or more players, several players
may be designated 'it' at the same time, playing with a single
ball that they may pass to each other; or each being given one
ball, they may throw it to one another to facilitate tagging.
Only that player who throws the ball that tags an opposing
player may change places with him.

Dodge ball

Ages: 6 and up.
Number of players: Two teams of 6 or more players each.
Equipment: Medium-sized inflated ball.
Place: Outdoors or gym.

Players are divided into two equal teams. One team forms a
circle large enough to allow the members of the second team
to move and run freely inside it. One member of the outside
circle team is given the ball. A time limit is set during which
each team serves as the circle team. For a game involving 6 to
10 members on each team, 3 to 5 minutes per innings is sufficient. The object of the game is for members of the outside
circle team to 'tag' inside team members with the ball. Circle
team members may pass the ball to each other before aiming
for inside team members. Any tagged inside team member
leaves the game.

Inside team members may move about and try to dodge the

ball. Circle team members may run into the circle only to recover the ball, but may not try to tag an inside team member with it until they have returned to their places on the outside circle. At the end of each innings, the tagged players who are out of the game are counted. That team wins which has tagged the largest number of opposing players at the end of the number of innings agreed upon.

Variation: Tagged players, instead of being out of the game, join the outside circle players for the rest of that innings. The last remaining inside player is the winner for his team.

School ball

Ages: 6 and older.
Number of players: 12 or more.
Equipment: One hollow rubber ball (or beanbag or balloon).
Place: Indoors (classroom or any other room, using beanbag or balloon only). Outdoors or gym (using any kind of medium-sized ball).

Players sit in rows on chairs or at their school desks or tables, or stand in line, one behind the other, or in a circle. The ball, beanbag, or balloon is never thrown, but passed by hand from one player to the next as rapidly as possible. Any player who fumbles and drops it is out of the game. (When played standing in a circle or in line, any player who is 'out' may be required to sit down in his place.) Each player must accept the ball and pass it on as rapidly as he can.

Played in a room or when all players are seated, the players close ranks or move up to adjacent seats as others drop out of the game. The last remaining player wins.

Variations (a large number of variations are possible in playing this game):
Number of players: 10 or more per team.
Place: Outdoors or gym.

1 Each team of players lines up in a single row, parallel to the next team. Or each team may form a circle. The first player in each row or circle holds one ball, bean bag, or balloon. At the word 'go' from the supervisor or from one player designated as the 'starter,' he passes (or throws) the ball to the next player, and so on down the line or around the circle. The last player in line (or the player who is the last next to the first player in a circle) runs to the head of the line (or runs once around the circle) and passes the ball to the next, in the same manner as did the first player. That team wins whose first player first returns with the ball to his original position.

2 Each team of players lines up in its own row, one behind the next, each straddling his legs as wide as possible. The first player passes the ball between his legs to the next, and so on down the line to the last player. The rest of the rules in (1) above remain the same.

3 Each team of players lines up in a row or in a circle. The players pass the ball backwards overhead from one to another. All other rules remain the same as in (1) above.

4 Two teams line up, each in a row, each 6 metres (20 feet) or more from a netball hoop (or a wastepaper basket, when the game is played by young children). The game is played as before, except that the last player in each row at each turn, must run to a marked line ahead of the basket, as soon as he receives the ball. He must then throw it and get it into the basket successfully. If he fails, he must keep trying until he has succeeded, and only then may he return with the ball to his place as the first in line, passing the ball back to the next player behind him, who passes it on until it is in the hands of the last player in line, who plays as did the first. The rest of the rules remain the same as in (1) above.

5 Two or more teams line up, each in a row, as before. The first member of each team stands at a marked place, 6 metres (20 feet) or more ahead of his line, facing the second player. He throws the ball to that player of his own team and then runs to the back of his line. The second player, on catching the

ball, runs to the marked place, faces his team, and throws the
ball to the player facing him, and so on. That team wins the
game whose first player to throw the ball stands once more at
the marked place, after all other team members have had their
turns. If either thrower or catcher drops the ball, that play
must be repeated.

6 Play begins as in (2) above. When the ball is passed back to
the last player in a row, all players about-face at his command.
They then pass the ball back to the first player, as before. That
team wins whose first player first receives the ball on completion of its passage in both directions.

7 Any of these games may be played with several balls, bean
bags, or balloons, used by each team at the same time. The last
player at his turn must wait until he has received as many balls
as are in play. All other rules remain the same as in (1) above.

Catch

Ages: 7 and older.
Number of players: 12 or more.
Equipment: Netball (or football, large inflated ball, beanbag, or
inflated balloon).
Place: Outdoors or gym.

All players but one form a circle. The remaining player stays
inside the circle. The players forming the circle pass the ball to
one another at random, being allowed to throw it from one
side of the ring to the other. The inside player tries to intercept
the ball or to knock it out of the hands of any other player. If
he succeeds, he then changes places with the last player to
touch or hold the ball. If any player who is part of the circle
drops the ball in the process of throwing or catching it,
whether or not this is due to interference from the inside
player, he also changes places with the inside player.

Variation 1: The same rules apply, except that all players must
kick the ball to each other and may not touch it with their
hands. A further variation that allows the inside player to

intercept the ball by both foot and hand is not recommended. It could lead to injury.

Variation 2 – PIGGY IN THE MIDDLE: 3 players. One is chosen to be the first 'pig.' The other two players stand about $2\frac{1}{2}$ to 3 metres (8 to 10 feet) apart. The 'pig' stands in the middle. The two outside players pass the ball back and forth between them by throwing or rolling it. The ball may not be thrown higher than the 'pig' can reach. When the 'pig' manages to intercept the ball he changes places with the player who threw it at that turn and the game continues as before. This can also be played as a running game in which all three players run while the ball is thrown and the 'pig' tries to catch it.

Variation 3: Any number of players. One is chosen by lot and given the ball. He throws it to any other player who is required to catch and throw it to another, and so on. Whenever a player fumbles and drops the ball or fails to catch it, he retrieves the ball, but then is required to stand on one leg while he throws it to another. He remains in that position for the rest of the game. A succession of similar penalties can be agreed on before the start of the game. The last remaining, unpenalized player is the winner.

Odd ball

Ages: 7 and older.
Number of players: 12 or more.
Equipment: Netball, football, or large inflated ball.
Place: Outdoors or gym.

All players but one form a circle, each with his feet spread apart as far as is comfortable. Each player's right foot touches the next player's left, all around the circle. The extra player is given the ball and goes into the centre of the circle. It is his object to throw (or kick) the ball out of the circle between players' legs. He may not throw (or kick) over the players' heads. The circle players may try to stop the ball with their hands, without moving the position of their feet. Any player among those forming the circle who loses his balance changes places with the centre player. If the centre player manages to throw (or kick) his ball outside the circle, he changes places with that player between whose legs the ball passed, or with the player to the right of the gap between the legs of 2 adjacent players, when the ball escapes the circle in this manner.

Variation: Instead of being placed in the centre, the extra player stays outside the circle and tries to throw (or kick) the ball into the circle, as before. All other rules remain the same.

Throw and go

Ages: 7 and older.

Number of players: 5 or more.

Equipment: Small or medium-sized rubber ball (or tennis ball); sticks (or tent pegs) – numbering one less than the number of players.

Place: Outdoors on soft ground.

Field: Lay out a circle at least 3 metres (10 feet) in diameter. Mark the centre of the circle. Make a number of holes, one less than the number of players, more or less evenly spaced around the circumference of the circle. Holes should be at least 1·5 metres (5 feet) apart, 7·5 cm (3 inches) deep, and about 10 cm (4 inches) in diameter.

The first player 'up' stands in the centre of the circle and holds the ball. Each of the rest of the players, with stick in hand, chooses one hole. Every player stands behind his hole, just outside the circle. At the word 'go' from the 'up' player in the middle, the rest race once around the circle until each returns to his original hole and places his stick into it.

As soon as he says 'go,' the 'up' player may throw or roll the ball, aiming for one of the holes. If the ball lands in an empty hole, the 'up' player changes places with the one whose hole it is. If the 'up' player misses, or if all players have their sticks in their holes on completion of their runs, or if the ball rolls into a hole in which a returned player has already placed his stick, the 'up' player must continue to resume play as before, to call 'go' and to throw his ball, until he succeeds in landing his ball in an empty hole.

Variation: STOOL BALL

Place: Indoors.

All the rules of 'throw and go' apply, except that players sit in a circle on stools or chairs. Instead of throwing his ball into a hole, the 'up' player tries to strike an unoccupied chair while its occupant races around the circle. This version of the game is very old, and probably originated in England. William Bradford, the five-times governor of Plymouth Colony, discovered children playing 'stool ball' one Christmas day, took away their ball, and henceforth prohibited all game-playing in the colony on this or any other holiday.

Chase ball

Ages: 8 and older.

Number of players: Any number, divided into two more or less equal teams.

Equipment: Football (or netball, or large, inflated rubber ball).

Place: Outdoors or gym.

This is an informal playground game in which players on the same team pass the ball back and forth to each other, while the opposing players try to intercept the ball and, if able to do so, pass it to members of their own team. This game is most frequently an informal school break game in which no scores are kept.

Centre ball

Ages: 8 and older.

Number of players: 10 or more.

Equipment: Netball, or large inflated ball.

Place: Outdoors or gym.

All players but one stretch out both arms to form a circle, in which each player stands at double arms' length from the next.

After the circle is formed, players lower their arms to a normal position. The odd player stands in the middle of the circle, holding the ball. He throws it at any player, and then runs outside the circle. The receiving player must catch it and run with it to the centre of the circle, where he puts it down. If he fails to catch the ball, he becomes the odd player, and the former odd player takes his place in the circle. If the receiving player catches the ball and places it in the centre, he must try to tag the odd player by hand before the latter can return to the middle of the circle and touch the ball. If the receiving player succeeds in tagging the odd player, the odd player must throw and run once more. If the odd player touches the ball in the centre before he is tagged, the receiving player then becomes the odd player. The game continues as before.

Piggyback ball
Ages: 10 and older.
Number of players: 12 or more.
Equipment: Football (or netball, inflated rubber ball, beanbag, or balloon).
Place: Outdoors on soft ground only.

The players are divided into two equal teams. One becomes the 'horse' team, the other the 'rider' team for the first innings. The horses carry the riders piggyback. One mounted rider is given the ball and must throw it to any other mounted rider, and so on. When any rider fumbles and drops the ball, all riders dismount at once and scatter. The nearest horse may then pick up the ball and throw it to any other horse or at any rider in order to tag him with it. The horses may attempt to tag a rider with only a single throw at their turn. If the horses fail to hit a rider, all riders remount, and the game continues as before. If a rider is tagged by a horse, then riders and horses change places and the horses mount the riders for the next innings, and so on.

AMERICAN INDIAN BALL GAMES

Lacrosse is the most famous American Indian ball game still played today. But the Indians of Florida once played a game that was a forerunner of today's basketball. A wicker basket was fixed to the top of a pole so that, when the ball was thrown into it properly, it turned around and around the pole. That player won who managed to turn the basket around the pole the largest number of times at a single throw.

The following are the rules for an ancient Indian game that can lead to rough scrimmages. Firm rules about allowable and disallowed body contact should be clearly spelled out, understood, and agreed to by all players before the start of the game.

Highball
Ages: 12 and older.
Number of players: 12 or more.

Equipment: Football (or netball, or large inflated ball); chalk.
Place: Outdoors.

A field, 18 metres by 6 metres (60 feet by 20 feet) or larger, is marked off and divided by a centre line at the halfway point (see diagram).

All players are grouped about the centre of the field. One player, chosen by lot, is given the ball. He throws it high into the air and tries to catch it as it returns. Any other player may catch the ball if he can. A player who catches the ball runs with it to score one point if he crosses the line at either end of the field while carrying the ball.

Any player may tackle the ball-carrier, according to the rules, and if he captures the ball, may try to score. A ball-carrying player may, if he feels himself threatened, pass the ball to any other player, whom he then pursues with the rest. Whenever a point is scored, the game resumes as it started, the scoring player being given the throw into the air. That player wins who scores the largest number of points within a time period agreed to before the start of the game.

BOWLS AND BOWLING

The modern game of bowls probably originated in Europe in the Middle Ages. The earliest known games were similar to the present-day Italian game of *Bocce*, in which one player throws out a small wood or metal ball. He, and then each additional player in turn, tries to bowl three larger balls as close to the first as possible. Only that player scores whose balls come closest to the first. And only those balls belonging to the winning player count that are closer to the first ball

than those of any other player. The medieval woodcut below shows that at that time the pins consisted of cones toward which players tossed or rolled their balls.

More 'pins' were added to these games until, in time, a variety of such games were standardized, among them our regulation bowling and curling-on-the-ice.

One example of how some of the seemingly meaningless

names of games originated is kayle-pins, an early form of nine-pins. It was later known as kettle, or kittle-pins, which eventually turned into the game of skittles.

Bowling-on-the-green, an English invention, was a game enthusiastically played by King Henry VIII. This version of the game led to the construction of indoor bowling alleys that soon became hangouts for criminals and dens of all sorts of skulduggery. Therefore, in the sixteenth century, King Henry's son, Edward VI, closed down all bowling alleys in England.

Among the games popular at the time was one called half-bowl. This game was played with one-half of a solid wooden bowling ball. It was delivered down a short, smooth alley towards a circle of 15 pins. The half-ball had to be spun so that it skittered around the circle of pins, entering the circle from the side away from the player, to knock down as many pins as possible.

About 1780, the magistrates of London once more banned bowling, citing the most popular games by name. This led to the revival of an older game, nine holes, one that the magistrates had neglected to specify in their edict. Players called it

bubble-the-justice, in the mistaken hope that they had out-
foxed the law.

Stake ball
Ages: 7 and older.
Number of players: 6 or more.
Equipment: Football (or netball, or large inflated ball); a set of
bowling pins (or skittles, large soda bottles, sticks, or tent
pegs) one less than the number of players; chalk or marking
stick.
Place: Indoors or outdoors.

Bowling pins (use sticks or tent pegs on soft ground) are set
up 3 to 4·5 metres (10 to 15 feet) apart. A circle, 1·2 metres
(4 feet) in diameter, is drawn or scratched around each bowling
pin. One player enters each circle containing a bowling pin.
The remaining player, chosen by lot, becomes 'it,' and may
stand anywhere, but must be at least 1·8 metres (6 feet) from
the nearest player at the start of the game. He is given the ball.
His object is to kick the ball so that it knocks down a bowling
pin (or hits a stick stuck into the ground). The players inside
their circles try to protect their own bowling pins as well as

they can, keeping at least one foot inside their own circles at all times. When 'it' knocks down a bowling pin, he changes places with the player in whose circle it stood. A player who leaves his circle, if spotted by 'it,' is challenged and becomes 'it,' changing places with his challenger.

Variation: This variation is played without bowling pins or

stakes. The object of 'it' is to tag a player who is outside his circle by throwing the ball at him. Players who beckon to each other may run and exchange circles. Each player who succeeds in doing so without being 'tagged' scores one point. A tagged player changes places with 'it' and becomes 'it,' until he has tagged another player outside his circle. That player wins who reaches a given score, or who has the highest score at the end of a time period agreed to before the start of the game.

Ball bowling

Ages: 7 and older.

Number of players: 1 or more.

Equipment: Football (or netball, or large inflated ball); 2 bowling pins (or skittles or empty soda bottles); chalk or tape.

Place: Indoors or outdoors.

The bowling pins are set up 4·5 metres (15 feet) or more from a starting line marked by tape or chalk. Bowling pins should be set up sufficiently far apart to allow the ball to pass between them (see diagram). The object is for each player, at his turn, to aim and roll the ball from the starting line so that it passes

between the two pins without knocking down either of them. Knocking down one pin and still rolling the ball between them costs a player 1 point. Rolling the ball between them and knocking down both pins costs him 2 points. Knocking down one pin, but failing to roll the ball between the two pins, costs a player 3 points. Failure to roll the ball between both pins and failure to knock down at least one pin costs him 4 points. That player wins who has the lowest score at the end of the number of innings agreed to before the beginning of the game.

Battle ball

Ages: 8 and older.

Number of players: Two teams of 5 or more players each.

Equipment: Football (or netball, or large inflated ball); as many bowling pins (or empty tin cans, or empty soda bottles) as the number of players; tape or chalk.

Place: Outdoors or gym.

A field, 12 metres by 4·5 metres (40 feet by 15 feet), is staked out. It is divided by a centre line halfway between the 12-metre (40-foot) lines, and two lines parallel to the centre line 1·2 metres (4 feet) from each end of the field (see diagram). Half the bowling pins (or whatever equipment is used) are placed, evenly spaced, at least 60 cm (2 feet) apart, in each end zone between the lines. In a game of more than 8 players per team, the pins should be lined up in two evenly spaced rows in each end zone.

Each team occupies and remains in one-half of the field. Players may not stand in the end zones or cross into them at any time during the game. If team captains are chosen, each

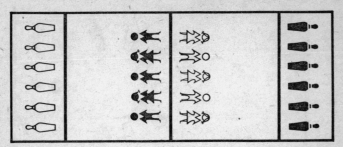

may place his players in positions he deems most advantageous. Each team in turn, in alternate innings, is given the ball for the first throw. The object of the game is for each team to knock down as many of the bowling pins as possible in the end zone of the opposing team by aiming the ball over the heads of or past the opponents. The ball may be passed among team members and intercepted by the opposing team. Each bowling pin knocked down counts one point. An innings may end either when all bowling pins of one side are knocked down, or at the end of a time period agreed to before the start of the game. That team wins which scores the largest number of points at the end of an even number of innings.

Variation: 2 or 4 balls may be used, equally divided between the teams at the beginning of the game.

Ricochet
Ages: 8 and older.
Number of players: 1 or more.
Equipment: Football (or netball, or large inflated ball); 10 bowling pins (or large empty soda bottles); chalk or tape.
Place: Indoors or outdoors.

All 10 bowling pins are set up in a circle, 1·5–1·8 metres (5–6 feet) from a wall, with room for the ball to pass between them. A starting line, about 6 metres (20 feet) from the wall and facing the circle of bowling pins, is marked with tape or chalk (see diagram overleaf).

Each player, at his turn, rolls or throws the ball against the wall so that it bounces or rolls back into the circle of bowling pins, knocking over as many as possible. Each pin downed at one turn scores one point for that player. Pins downed *before* the ball has hit the wall score against that player, each downed pin counting as minus one point. Pins are set up again between each player's turn. That player wins who scores highest in the number of innings agreed to before the start of the game.

BALL GAMES WITH STICKS, BATS, MALLETS, OR RACKETS

The earliest version of golf, played with a small, hard ball made of leather stuffed with feathers, was known in the days of ancient Rome. It was driven by players armed with a club that was curved at one end. The medieval game of Goff gave the modern one its name. Rules similar to those for Goff applied to a game called Bandy Ball in the fourteenth century, and to Stow Ball, popular in Europe in the sixteenth and seventeenth centuries.

Polo, played by teams of horsemen who try to score goals by driving a puck with mallets, originated centuries ago in Persia, where such a game was played with rackets and a hard leather ball. This game, like the jousting tournament of armoured knights, though a mock battle, was taken most seriously by its players. And a similar game is still played by today's Afghan tribesmen. They compete for possession of the body of a beheaded calf, with which they score by carrying it on horseback across a goal line.

The ancestors of modern croquet were the seventeenth-century game of Pall-Mall, and an earlier one called Ring Ball, both of which originated in England.

Club Ball, first recorded in 1344, was the forerunner of rounders, which led to the rules and methods of play for

baseball. The game of cricket shares the same beginnings.

The game that gave birth to tennis, badminton, and squash was probably first played in France without a racket. The ball was struck with the open palm – sometimes heavily gloved, at other times bare. In 1424, a French woman named Margot was a champion of this game. Played with rackets, tennis became a favourite among the nobility of Europe. The ledgers of England's King Henry VII testify that players, then as now, lost balls that they drove outside the courts: 'Item for the king's loss at tennis, twelvepence; for the loss of balls, three-pence.'

Trap ball

Ages: 9 and older.

Number of players: 2 or more.

Equipment: Soft, small rubber ball (or tennis ball); rounders bat (or stick); 1 trap (see illustration).

Place: Outdoors.

A circle, 6 metres (20 feet) or more in diameter, is marked around the trap in the centre. The first player, chosen by lot, steps up to the trap with a bat in hand. He strikes the trap with his bat, releasing the ball. He must hit the ball with his bat while it is in the air. The rest of the players stay outside this

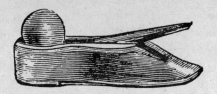

circle. If the player up at bat fails 3 times in a row to strike the ball outside the circle, or if he strikes the ball outside the circle, but it is caught by one of the other players before it falls to the ground, he loses his turn either to the next batter chosen by lot, or to the player who caught the ball.

If the batter hits the ball outside the circle and no one catches it before it strikes the ground, he scores 1 point and continues at bat until he either misses 3 turns at bat in succession, or is caught out. The highest-scoring player wins after all players have had their turns at bat.

Variation 1: The batter drops his bat on the ground as soon as he has hit the ball beyond the circle. If the ball is not caught, the player who picks it off the ground may throw it at the bat inside the circle, from the spot at which he picked up the ball. If he hits the bat, or if it is agreed that he need only come within 60 cm (2 feet) of the bat, the batter is 'out,' and that player becomes the next batter 'up.'

Variation 2: The ball may be thrown by a player, chosen by lot, if no trap is available. Only the thrower may catch the ball, *inside the circle*, and, if he is able to do so before the struck ball hits the ground, may take his turn at bat. The other players must stay outside the circle, but may catch the batter out, as in the original game.

Hand tennis
Ages: 12 and older.
Number of players: 2, or two teams of 2 players each.
Equipment: Fives ball or golf ball, and 1 padded glove for each player (or a small, soft hollow rubber ball or tennis ball that can be struck with the ungloved hand).

Place: Indoor court or an area enclosed by a two- or three-sided windowless wall, at least 4·5 metres (15 feet) high, marked by a line at the players' chest height.

This game is played in England as the formal game of Fives; but when played against a single wall, it is much like Handball. The first player, chosen by lot, throws the ball up into the air and bats it with his hand against the wall (in a single-wall game); or into a corner above the marked line, so that it first strikes both walls before bouncing onto the ground (in a court with more than one wall). The second player, or one member of the second team, must similarly bat the ball with his hand before it bounces, or before it bounces more than once on the ground, letting it strike one or more walls above the line before it falls to the ground. The game continues until one player misses returning the ball before it strikes the ground twice. Each such 'miss' scores 1 point for the opponent or for the opposing team. That player or team wins which first scores 21 points.

BALL GAMES THAT REQUIRE MARKED COURTS OR PLAYING FIELDS

Prehistoric men undoubtedly found that throwing or other skills required for their own or for tribal defence or support could be practised in play. But I doubt that they could play formal games until they were able to understand 'that their struggles with nature, with predators and with other men were not haphazard encounters. They [first] had to discover that there was a possibility of design and of planning for the exigencies of daily life. Once man realized that he was not just a plaything of chance, he could begin to plan his moves, foresee probable results, and take luck into account as one of the components.

'Man probably did not take long to discover how to scratch his plan into the soft earth, using sticks or pebbles to show the position of hunters and prey, attackers and defenders.' Early man may also have deduced the need for rules from a recognition of this possibility of planning. 'And so the first game [using a playing field] may have been invented.'[2] Eventually, tribal chiefs may have thought of the idea of using live men in planning these strategies. It is a small step from this kind of planning to making the men act out their roles in mock combat or hunt. Within historical times, the princes and maharajas of India played chess and Pachisi in this manner, laying out life-sized game boards in the courtyards of their palaces. Many of these games became a part of religious ritual, in which the stakes sometimes were a matter of life and death for the participants.

The following ball games, descendants of these early games, require playing fields that can be improvised indoors and out, using tape or ribbons, chalk lines, or sticks and stones to mark boundaries and goals.

Balloon ball

Ages: 6 and older.
Number of players: Two teams of 6 or more players each.
Equipment: Balloon; tape (or string or twine).
Place: Indoors in classroom or any other room.

Two lengths of string, tape, ribbon, or twine are strung 1·8 metres (6 feet) from the floor, from wall to wall, one at each end of the room, 60 cm (2 feet) from end walls, with sufficient room left for both teams to stand or sit, evenly distributed, facing each other, in the centre of the room (see diagram).

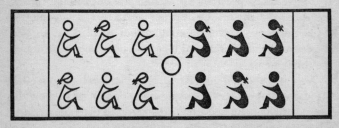

The balloon is tossed into the centre of the room. The object of the game is for teams to score by slapping the balloon across the opponents' goal (as represented by the ribbon *behind* each team). Each time the balloon drifts between the ribbon and the wall, it scores 1 goal for the opposing team. That team wins which scores the greatest number of goals in a given time period, or that first reaches a number of goals agreed to before the start of the game. At the scoring of a goal, the game resumes as at first.

Variation 1: The ribbons may be strung across the four corners of the room, two belonging to each team (see diagram). All other rules remain as before.

Variation 2:
Ages: 7 and older.
Number of players: Two teams of 8 or more players each.
Place: Outdoors or gym.

A field, 6 by 9 metres (20 by 30 feet) (or larger, depending on the ages and number of players), is marked out and divided by

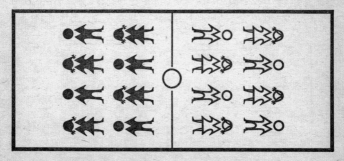

a centre line halfway at the 9-metre (30-foot) lines (see diagram on page 63).

Each team lines up facing the other, about 30 cm (1 foot) from the centre line (see diagram). The balloon is tossed into the centre, between both teams, who then try, by striking it, to drive it across the line marking the end zone of the opposing team. Team members may cross into each other's territory, once the balloon is released among them. It may never be carried in the hand or held, but must at all times be struck or pushed. Each time the balloon crosses the end zone on one side or the other, the opposing team scores, and play resumes as at first, both teams lining up at the centre line, the team that scored the last point being given the balloon. That team wins which scores the largest number of points in a time period, or achieves a point score agreed to before the start of the game.

Roll ball

Ages: 7 and older.
Number of players: 6 or more.
Equipment: Small, bouncing rubber ball; 5 pebbles (or bottle caps) for each player; metal spoons for digging.
Place: Outdoors on soft ground.

Players line up as closely as possible, in a single line. Each digs a hole at his feet, about half again as large and half as deep as the circumference of the ball to be used. A line is marked, 3 metres (10 feet) (or more for older players) away from, but centred on, the line of holes (see diagram).

One player, chosen by lot, leaves his hole and stands at the mark. The rest of the players stay behind their respective holes. The first 'up' player tries to roll the ball into any of the holes. The player into whose hole the ball rolled (even if it is the ball-roller's own) must pick it up. The rest of the players scatter. The player who picked up the ball now tries to 'tag' any other player by throwing the ball at him. A tagged player must place one of his pebbles into his own hole, and then take his turn at the mark as the next ball-roller.

If the player into whose hole the ball rolls fails to tag another player, he places one of his pebbles in his own hole and takes his turn at the mark. As soon as any player has placed the fifth pebble in his own hole, he is out of the game. That player wins who stays in the game longest.

Hole ball

Ages: 7 and older.
Number of players: 1 or more.
Equipment: Cricket ball (or small, rubber ball); small digging tool (or metal spoon).
Place: Outdoors on soft ground.

Using your own shoe length as a 30 cm (1-foot) measure, pace out a straight line about 12 metres (42 feet) long. Mark a starting point at one end of the line. Then dig a hole, 7·5 or 10 cm (3 or 4 inches) deep and half again as wide, 3 metres (10 feet) from the starting point. Another hole is dug, 1·2 metres (4 feet) from the first, then three others, each spaced out 2·5 metres (8 feet) from one another, all along the line (see diagram).

The first player bowls the ball from the starting point to the

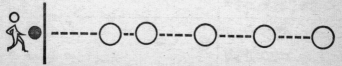

first hole. If he manages to sink the ball into the first hole, he may continue by lifting the ball out of the hole and bowling from that hole to the next, and so on. He loses his turn at any hole in which he fails to sink the ball on the first try (or more, if agreed to before the start of the game). Each player scores according to the number of holes he successfully fills with his ball at successive innings. That player wins who has the highest score at the end of the number of innings agreed to before the start of the game.

Relay ball
Ages: 8 and older.
Number of players: 12 or more for each of two even-numbered teams.
Equipment: 2 footballs (or netballs, or large inflated balls); tape or chalk.
Place: Outdoors or gym.

A field is staked out as shown (see diagram). Each team is divided into two equal groups and lined up as shown (see diagram). The first player in one of each team's lines is given a ball. At the signal to start, the two first-in-line players of each team race toward the other end of the field, tossing the ball from one to the other. On reaching (touching with one foot or crossing) the end line, both players of each team return, continuing to pass the ball between them as before. The ball must be passed at least 4 times on each lap.

On their return to the starting line, whichever player has the ball at that time passes it to one of the next two team members,

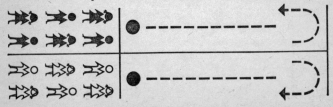

who continue the game as before, and each then stands last in his respective line. That team wins whose first two players first stand at the head of their respective lines again, after all other players have run the course.

Variation: This game can be played so that the ball is kicked between players, but never touched by hand.

Corner goal ball

Ages: 9 and older.
Number of players: 6 or more for each of two teams.
Equipment: Football (or netball, or large inflated ball).
Place: Outdoors or gym.

A field, 7·5 by 12 metres (25 by 40 feet), is staked out and divided by a centre line into halves, each 7·5 by 6 metres (25 by 20 feet). 1·2 metre (4-foot) squares, one at each corner of the field, serve as goals (see diagram).

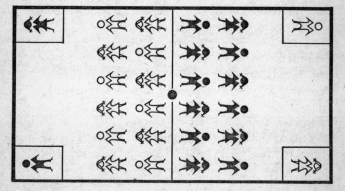

All but 2 players of each team line up 1·2 metres (4 feet) from, and on opposite sides of, the centre line. The 2 remaining players on each team stand, one each, in the corner goals in the half of the playing field occupied by the opposing team (see diagram). The ball is given to one member of whichever team is chosen by lot to begin the game. The object is to throw the ball over the heads of the opposing team to one of the two goalkeepers who are members of the throwing team. The opposing team tries to intercept the ball and scores in the same manner.

Goalkeepers may step beyond their goals, provided they keep one hand (or foot) inside the goal. Each time a goalkeeper captures the ball, he scores 1 point for his team. He then tries to throw the ball back to his own team. Team members may pass the ball to each other, and may intercept the throw from the goalkeeper to his own team, provided they do not reach or step inside the goal lines or into the opposing team's half of the playing field. The winning team is the one with the highest score at the end of a given time period.

The game can also be played so that the team wins which first scores 20 (or more, or less) points.

Variation: Agreement is made before the game about whether players may or may not wrest the ball from a goalkeeper who has captured it, before he touches the ground inside his goal with the ball in order to score.

Rounders
Ages: 9 and older.
Number of players: Two teams of 9 players each for the conventional game; more players can be added to each team, up to a total of 12 or 14 players per team.
Equipment: Rounders ball or tennis ball; rounders bat (or stick); tape or chalk.
Place: Outdoors.

A five-sided field is marked off, 7·5 metres (25 feet) per side, with bases at four of the corners. Home base is marked at the fifth corner; a bowler's line is drawn 3·6 metres (12 feet) from base (see diagram).

The players are divided into two teams, a member of each tossing for first side to bat. The fielding team selects a bowler

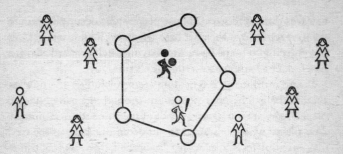

for the first innings, and the batting side tosses to determine batting order.

The fielders stand at various locations, outside the field of play. One stands behind the batter as backstop, to retrieve missed balls. No fielder may stand between the bowler and the batter. The batter stands next to home base. The bowler throws the ball underarm. The player batting may refuse any ball; but if he tries to hit a ball, it counts as one of the three tries to which he is entitled. If he fails to hit the ball after three tries, he is 'out.' If he hits a ball, he must drop his bat and run to his right to the first corner base, or beyond if he thinks that he can successfully reach second, third, fourth, or home base, and if these are unoccupied.

Only one batter at a time may occupy any single base. When a batter has hit the ball, the man on second base must run

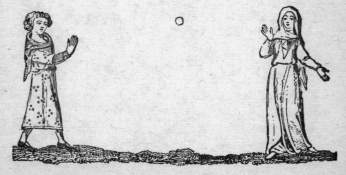

towards third, and so on. Those players who occupy bases must try to reach at least the next base whenever a hit is made. Only by returning to home base, after having safely reached all other bases, does a batter score a run for his side.

If any member of the fielding team, including the bowler, catches the ball before it strikes the ground, the batter, and all players who are 'off' base, are out of the game for that innings. Any player who has started to run from one base to the next may attempt to return to his last base before such a ball is caught. Any fielder may throw the ball and try to hit a runner with it. If the ball hits the batter, or any other runner who is between bases, before he reaches a base or has one foot on it, that batter or runner is also out of the game. Fielders may throw the ball to each other and to the pitcher to try to tag any batter running between bases. They may also chase a runner and tag him by touching him with the ball. However, no fielder may catch and hold a runner so that another fielder may tag him.

When all members of the team batting first have completed

their turns, whether or not they occupy bases, that innings ends and the teams switch sides. The game continues as before. That team wins which has scored the largest number of runs during its innings, or after the number of innings agreed to before the start of the game.

Variation: Players should decide before the game whether base-stealing (running from base before the batter hits the ball) is allowed, when the next base is unoccupied.

2
Marble Games

The children of ancient Rome used nuts for playing games similar to some of the marble games described here. Originally, these were children's versions of bowling games they saw their elders play. As these games became popular, special marbles were made for young players, first of stone and clay, later of marble, agate, and glass. Devotees have invented a long list of names for the various kinds, ranging from 'bosses,' 'bonzes,' 'aggies,' 'glassies,' 'alleys,' 'baries,' 'poppos,' and 'stonies,' to 'taws.' Marble game crazes have waxed and waned periodically. During one of the peak periods in England, around 1860, an anonymous Victorian described marbles rapturously as 'glass spheres holding a twisted spiral of filament, thin music translated into coloured glass, crimson with pale blue, fire with Canary, emerald with rose. The similar sphere of the eye, however juxtaposed to the harder crystal, peers in vain through the twisted colours to see a heart.'

Shooting marbles requires a certain amount of skill and con-centration, the symptoms of which one can see in the little boy scrunched close to the ground, marble in hand, poised to shoot, eyes fixed on the target, neck stretched, chin out and teeth clenched over the lower lip. I recall the passion with which these games were played in my childhood. A gaming fever possessed us, born of greed or despair as one's hoard swelled or shrank inside the little marble bag each of us clutched to himself with miserly mania.

In the first half of this century, marble playing was taken sufficiently seriously that an Official Set of State and Interstate Rules was drawn up by a Conference of American Recreation Executives from 60 New Jersey and Pennsylvania cities. I can imagine these paunchy, middle-aged men, thrashing out, com-promising and settling, in smoke-filled caucus, the 31 rules for the official game of marbles, in addition to a set of definitions of terms that include: ' "Hysting," – the act of raising the

hand from the ground in shooting (Forbidden).' So, no hysting, please.

The following marble games and their rules have been distilled and adapted from those most popular in the past. Any of these games can be played, won, or lost according to one of two ways. The first depends on a winning score based on the number of points scored or games won, in which captured marbles are returned to every player at the end of each game. The second, in which some players may 'lose all their marbles,' is a game of 'winner take all,' or at least as many as he can capture. The first kind of game is for fun, the second 'for keeps,' or 'in earnest.' I recommend the former for children below school age and for any who cannot stand losing their treasured marbles. And of course, children should be encouraged to adapt the given rules in any way on which they can agree.

In many marble games, players shoot from a mark, called the 'taw,' some distance from their targets. A 1·2 to 1·8-metre (4 to 6-foot) distance is ample for preschool children. But the

distances can be increased for games played by older and more skilled players. The established manner of shooting marbles consists of holding the marble in the hollow made by pressing the thumb against the forefinger, 2·5 cm (1 inch) or so off the ground, and flicking the thumb to propel the little ball forward. This is called 'knuckling down' (see illustration below).

A less favoured method is to rest the marble on the floor or the ground and to flick it with the forefinger toward its target.

Some of the games depend for their outcome on how close a player can bring his marble to a target or to an opponent's marble. Such games are difficult for smaller children or when played on rough ground. The rules may be adapted so that the winning player is the one whose marble comes within a 'span' of his target, or closer – a span being that player's hand's breadth, with fingers stretched out, from the tip of the thumb to the end of the little finger.

The order in which players shoot their marbles is most often decided by each player's throwing or shooting one marble

toward a marked line or circle, the nearest to the line or the closest to the centre of the circle being first, the next closest second, and so on.

Bounce eye
Ages: 5 and older.
Number of players: 2 or more.
Equipment: An equal number of marbles for each player; chalk or stick for marking lines.
Place: Indoors or outdoors.

A circle about 30 cm (1 foot) in diameter is drawn on the ground or the floor. Each player places 2 or more marbles in a heap in the centre of the circle. Each player in turn stands close to the circle and drops one of his other marbles straight down, from eye-level height. His object is to aim this marble so that it strikes the largest number of marbles and knocks them out of the circle. After the drop, the player captures any marbles which he has knocked outside the circle, and recovers his shooter. If he fails to knock any marbles out, his shooter is added to those remaining in the circle. The game ends when no marbles remain in the circle.

Marble shoot

Ages: 6 and older.
Number of players: Any number.
Equipment: An equal number of marbles, all of the same size, for each player; chalk or stick for marking line.
Place: Indoors or outdoors.

A starting line is marked on the floor or the ground with chalk or a stick. The first shooter, chosen by lot, shoots out his marble from behind the starting line. The second player shoots his marble in the same manner, attempting to hit the first player's marble. If he succeeds, he pockets both the opponent's marble and his own. If he fails, the third player (or the first, in a game of only 2 players) aims for either marble, and, if he strikes one, may continue until he misses or until he has captured all marbles on the field. If no marble remains on the ground, the next player shoots out a marble and the game continues as at first. That player wins who captures the largest number of his opponents' marbles.

Variation 1: On agreement before the game, the second player captures the first player's marble if his shot comes within a 'span' of it.

Variation 2: The target consists of 4 marbles arranged as shown (see diagram overleaf), 3 marbles touching, set out in a triangle, forming the base for a fourth, placed on top. This is the 'castle.' Each player in turn builds a castle with his own marbles for the next player. If the shooter hits the target from a given distance and dislodges the top marble, he captures all 4. If he fails to do so, he loses his shooter to the player who built the castle.

Variation 3: The 'castle' can also be constructed by placing a regular playing die on top of the foundation. If a player fails to dislodge the die, he forfeits his shooter to the player who built the castle. If he hits the castle, the player who built the castle pays him as many marbles as the number shown uppermost on the die after it has rolled off.

Variation 4: A large 'castle' can be made by placing 9 marbles at the base, then 6, then 4, and then 1 (or a die) on top.

Variation 5: The 'keeper' method used in Marble Bridge (see p. 83) can be employed in these 'castle' games. The castle-keeper is selected and 'pays' according to the number of marbles scattered beyond a small circle. The 'keeper' wins the shooter of any player who fails to score.

Target

Ages: 6 and older.

Number of players: Any number.

Equipment: An equal number of marbles, all of the same size, for each player; chalk or stick for marking line.

Place: Indoors or outdoors.

A shooting line is marked on the floor or the ground with chalk or a stick. Each player contributes a given number (3 to 6) of his own marbles, which he sets up, along with an equal number from each other player, in a circle or row, at a distance from the shooting line. Each player in turn shoots one marble into this target. A player takes as many marbles as he hits at his turn, and recovers his own shooter. If he fails to hit any, he leaves his shooter where it came to rest. That player wins who captures the largest number of marbles in the number of turns agreed to before the start of the game.

Ring game
Ages: 6 and older.
Number of players: Any number.
Equipment: An equal number of marbles, all of the same size, for each player; chalk or stick for marking line.
Place: Indoors or outdoors.

A shooting line is marked on the ground or the floor with chalk or stick. Each player contributes an equal number of marbles to make up a circle of 16 or more marbles, set up with plenty of space between them. A larger marble or target is set in the centre. The first player, chosen by lot, shoots from the shooting line, marked some distance from the circle, and tries to hit the centre target. If he fails to do so, his shooter remains where it lies. If he succeeds in hitting the target, he may then try to hit any of the marbles set up in the circumference of the

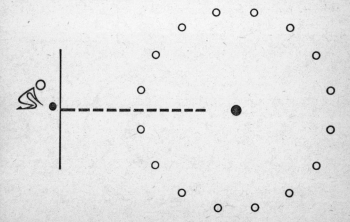

circle, by shooting his marble from where it lies. He collects any marble he hits, other than the centre marble, and removes it from the game. He continues shooting, from wherever his shooter lands, for as long as he hits and pockets another marble. His turn ends when he fails to hit another marble. Each player takes his turn in the same manner. Any player may also aim for any shooter marbles left in the ring by previous players. Or he may win shooters outside the ring by hitting them. When all marbles, except the target, have been won, each player again contributes an equal number for the next game. A new first player is selected, and the game resumes as before.

Shoot out

Ages: 7 and older.
Number of players: Any number.
Equipment: An equal number of marbles, all of the same size, for each player; chalk or stick for marking line.
Place: Indoors or outdoors.

A large circle, 90 cm (3 feet) or more in diameter, is drawn on the floor or the ground. A smaller circle, 10 to 12·5 cm (4 to 5 inches) in diameter, is drawn in the centre of the large one. Each player places an equal number of marbles inside the small circle. Players shoot from the edge of the large circle, and may not extend their hands inside it to play. Each player (using his

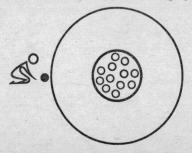

remaining marbles) tries to shoot as many of the marbles as possible out of the large circle. Each player shoots in turn, continuing to shoot from where his shooter lands, for as long as he fires at least one marble outside the large circle. When a player fails to shoot any other marble out of the large circle at his turn, even if his shooter has gone outside the large circle, play passes to the next player, and so on. Any player's shooter marble left in the large circle at the end of his turn may be shot out by following players or by himself, at his next turn. A player captures all marbles which he shoots outside the large circle. Play continues until all marbles have been captured.

Marble bocce

Ages: 7 and older.
Number of players: 2 or more.
Equipment: Each player should have 6 marbles of the same colour, and each player's colour should be different; 1 large target marble; chalk or stick for marking line.
Place: Indoors or outdoors.

The first player shoots out the large target marble from a marked starting line. He then shoots one of his marbles, trying to come as close to the target marble as possible. Each player shoots one marble in turn, until all have played their 6 marbles. A player may dislodge the target marble or any other player's marbles, or even his own that he previously shot. The player's object is to try to get as many as possible of his marbles closer to the target than those of any other player. After every player has shot all 6 marbles, the player whose marble lies closest to the target is the only one who scores. He receives 1 point for that marble, and 1 point for every other marble that lies closer to the target than any opponent's marble does. The player who first scores 21 or more points in succeeding games is the winner.

Variation 1: The target marble is placed 15 cm (6 inches) from a wall. All rules remain the same, except that each player's marbles must be shot against the wall and bounce off it, before coming to a halt as close to the target as possible. A shooter marble that comes to rest before it hits the wall is removed from the game at once. That player loses his turn and may not shoot that marble during that innings.

Variation 2: Instead of setting out a target marble, players draw a line some distance from a shooting line from which all players shoot. That player who comes closest to the line in successive turns wins all the marbles.

Variation 3: Lean a flat board against a wall. Each player in turn rolls his marble down the board toward the target marble. All other rules remain the same.

Nine holes

Ages: 7 and older.
Number of players: 2 or more.
Equipment: An equal number of marbles for each player; equipment for digging holes in ground; stick for marking line.
Place: Outdoors on soft ground.

Three rows of 3 small holes each are dug in the ground, forming a square. Each hole should be an equal distance (15 to 22 cm or 6 to 9 inches) from each adjacent hole (see diagram). Each hole should be large enough to hold 6 to 8 marbles. Each player contributes an equal number of marbles, so that

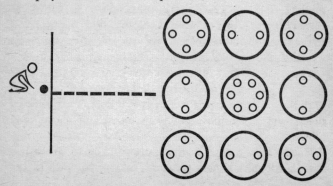

the centre hole contains the most marbles, and twice as many marbles are in each of the 4 corner holes as are in any of the remaining 4. For example, if there are 3 players, each may contribute 10 marbles. Four marbles are placed in each corner hole, 2 in each of the other 4 outside holes, and 6 in the middle.

Players shoot from a line marked a given distance from the holes. Each player in turn aims 1 marble per turn towards the holes. If his marble falls into a hole, he captures all marbles in it. If he misses landing his shooter in a hole, it is added to the store in the nearest hole. If a marble lands exactly between holes, or if the nearest hole is too full, then it is placed into any empty hole, or into that hole containing the least number of marbles. If, after the beginning of the game, a player's shooter lands in an empty hole, he must add as many marbles from his own stock as that hole contained at the beginning of the game. The game ends when all holes are empty. The player who captures the largest number of marbles is the winner.

Marble bridge
Ages: 7 and older.
Number of players: 2 or more.
Equipment: 3 marbles for each player; an arched bridge, cut out from cardboard, containing 9 or more holes (see illustration). Arches should be cut large enough for marbles to go through. Each arch is numbered at random. Chalk or stick for marking line.
Place: Indoors or outdoors.

Players shoot from a marked line, a given distance from the bridge. Each player shoots all three of his marbles at each turn. A marble scores only if it passes all the way through an arch. The sum of the numbers over the arches through which he is able to shoot his marbles is the player's score at that turn. The winner is the player who has the highest score at the end of a number of turns agreed to before the start of the game.

Variation: Each player starts with an equal number of marbles. One player is chosen 'bridge-keeper' by lot. Each player in turn shoots one marble at the bridge. If he scores by shooting his marble through one of the arches, the bridge-keeper must 'pay' him the number written over that arch. If he misses, he surrenders his shooter to the bridge-keeper. After each player has shot his marble, he who shot first becomes bridge-keeper, and so on until all players have had their turns.

Picking the plums

Ages: 7 and older.
Number of players: 2, or two teams of up to 4 players each.
Equipment: An equal number of 'target' marbles for each player or team, plus 3 'shooter' marbles per player or team; chalk or stick for marking lines.
Place: Indoors or outdoors.

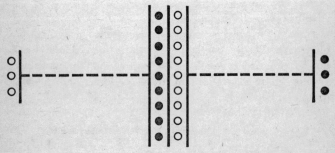

Three parallel lines, 1·2 metres (4 feet) long and 12 cm (8 inches) apart, are drawn on the floor (or scratched lightly into the ground); the shooting lines for each player or team are determined by one player's starting from the centre line and pacing off an equal number of steps (12 or more) in each direction. Each side sets up its target marbles between the centre line and the outside line closest to the opponent.

Each player (or each team's players in turn) fires 3 marbles at the target marbles of the opponent. The opposing players or teams take turns shooting. The object is for each player to shoot the opponent's target marbles across the centre line. A player or team captures any opponent's target marble which is moved across the centre line and removes it. Each player or team recovers its own 3 shooter marbles between turns. The game ends when one player or team has captured all of the opponent's target marbles.

Variation: Only two parallel lines are drawn. Each player contributes an equal number of marbles to be set up in a straight row between the lines. Players shoot from opposite sides, capturing marbles they shoot beyond the line facing the opponent.

3
Button Games

Many of the marble games listed in the previous section can also be adapted to be played with buttons that are tossed, rolled on their edges, or snapped, one against another, as in the game of Tiddlywinks (see illustration) (see Marble Games: Marble Shoot; Target; Nine Holes, etc.). The following button games are especially useful at parties or on occasions when no other materials for play are at hand. Flat stones or coins can be substituted for buttons in many of these games.

Buttons also lend themselves to making an instant toy that was popular over one hundred years ago, but is unknown to many contemporary children. Required materials are a button that has at least two holes in it, and a thread or thin string, 60 to 75 cm (24 to 30 inches) long. Thread the button through one hole in one direction and through the second in the other (see illustration) and tie the ends of the thread together. If the child puts the forefinger of each hand through the loops, one

finger on each side of the button, and twists the string a few times, he can make the button spin rapidly back and forth, by alternately pulling and relaxing his hold on the string. If the button is large enough, it will make a humming sound. The same toy can be made by cutting a cardboard disc and punching two holes in it, 3 mm ($\frac{1}{8}$ inch) apart, on both sides of the centre.

Button-stringing contest
Ages: 4 and older.
Number of players: 2 or more.
Equipment: An equal number of large buttons with large holes for each player; 1 length of light string or thread on which buttons can be strung without difficulty; 1 button is tied to the end of each string or thread.
Place: Indoors.

Each player tries to string his buttons as quickly as possible. This game can be played for a given period of time, allowing each player to string, unstring, and restring all of his buttons several times in succession. The winner is the player who is able to do this the greatest number of times in the set time period.

Knock 'em down
Ages: 6 and older.
Number of players: 1 or more.
Equipment: 1 medium-sized button (or a coin or flat stone); 1 wooden stake or stick, sufficiently flat at one end so that the button can be balanced on it; an equal number of pebbles for each player (or sticks, each 6 inches – 15 cm – long).

Place: Outdoors on soft ground.

A circle, 60 to 90 cm (2 to 3 feet) in diameter, is marked on the ground; the stake is set in the centre, with the button balanced on top of it; a line is marked 1·8 metres (6 feet) from the stake (or further for older players).

Standing at the mark, each player in turn throws his pebbles or the short stick at the button, and tries to knock it off the top of the stake so that it falls outside the circle. The winner is the player who succeeds the most times in a given number of turns. The objective, of course, is to aim at the top of the stake.

Tiddlywinks or snip-snap
Ages: 6 or older.
Number of players: 2 or more.
Equipment: 3 medium-sized buttons or counters each (preferably all of the same size, but a different colour for each player); 1 large button or counter; chalk or stick for marking lines.
Place: Indoors or outdoors.

A starting line and a finishing line are marked, 2·5 to 3 metres (8 to 10 feet) apart.

Each player lines up his buttons at the starting line, next to those of the other player or players. Then each player in turn, using the large button, snaps his own buttons towards the finishing line. If one player manages to snap his button so that it falls on and partially covers an opponent's button in front of the finishing line, he captures that button. That player wins who first reaches the finishing line with the largest number of his buttons.

Variation: This same game can be played using a hole, rather than a finishing line, as the target.

Snap pebble

Ages: 6 or older.
Number of players: 2 or more.

Equipment: 10 or more small, flat buttons or stones; chalk or small stick.
Place: Indoors or outdoors.

One player scatters the buttons or pebbles on the ground. The first player, chosen by lot, draws a line (with chalk or stick) between any 2 buttons. He then flicks 1 of these 2 buttons with his index finger across the line, trying to hit the other. If he succeeds he takes the struck button out of the game, draws another line, anywhere between any 2 remaining buttons, and continues as before. He loses his turn only when he fails to hit another button for which he aims. The second player then takes his place and the game continues in turn. That player wins who has collected the largest number of buttons when only a single button is left on the ground.

London

Ages: 7 and older.
Number of players: 2 or more.
Equipment: Large sheet of brown wrapping paper, 75 × 90 cm (30 × 35 inches) or larger; chalk; crayon or stick; 2 large buttons, or one marble, ping-pong ball or small ball made of wadded tissue paper.
Place: Indoors or outdoors.

If played indoors, tape the wrapping paper onto the floor. On it, draw the diagram shown below, using either crayon or chalk. Out of doors, scratch the same diagram into soft ground or draw it, using chalk, on pavement.

The first player kneels before the base line of the diagram and propels his playing piece in the following manner. If buttons are used, snap one against the other; if a marble is used, flick it with an index finger; if a ping-pong ball or a tissue ball is used, blow on it, or flick it like the marble.

A player loses his turn when his playing piece lands on a line or outside the game diagram. If it lands on a space between the lines, he draws a small circle in that space, marks it with his initial, and resumes play as before until he loses his turn. If the playing piece lands in a space that is occupied by a circle with his initial in it, at any turn, he draws a small oval under the circle (see diagram), next one leg, and thereafter another, each time his counter lands in that same space. The first player to complete three such armless figures in any space, draws in the arms at that turn and 'owns' it (see diagram) no

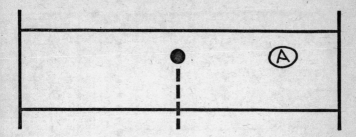

matter how many incomplete figures, drawn by other players, occupy it. Any other player who, in his turn, lands in such an 'owned' space, loses his turn.

Players may only add to or complete their own figures on landing on any space in their respective turns. Whenever a player lands on 'London' he may, at that turn, add one feature to any one of his own figures that occupies any space on the diagram, including drawing the arms of a completed set of three or starting a new one in any space that is not yet 'owned.' That player wins who 'owns' the greatest number of spaces when all are 'owned.'

Toss-up

Ages: 8 and older.

Number of players: 2 or more.

Equipment: An equal number of buttons for each player (each player should have a different colour, if possible); 1 large button or pebble, used as a target; stick for marking line.

Place: Outdoors, against a windowless wall.

A mark is made 1·8 to 3 metres (6 to 10 feet) from the wall.

The first player, chosen by lot, stands at the mark and tosses the target button or pebble so that it bounces off the wall and lands a distance away from it. He then begins the first round, in which each player in turn stands at the mark and bounces one of his own buttons off the wall. The object is to make the button land within a 'span' (see Marble Games introduction) of the target. The player who comes closest wins all the other buttons thrown in that round. If no player comes within a 'span' of the target, players continue for another round, leaving the target and all previously thrown buttons in place. Otherwise a new round is started like the first, the target button being rethrown for each round, the second player in the first round becoming the first in the second, and so on.

If any player's button does not strike the wall before it lands, that player is disqualified from winning the round, even if his button comes closest to the target. His button is captured, along with the rest, by the winner of that round.

4
Hop, Skip and Jump

In an era when most children spend a great deal of time sitting
– on school buses, in school, at home in front of their TV sets,
radios and record players, in cinemas and, at later ages, in cars –
it seems a good idea to keep their circulation going from
earliest ages on, by encouraging vigorous exercise in play. The
following games have been selected because of their relative
informality and the few, if any, materials that are needed to
play them. Further, these are games that do not require large
teams. Two or more children can play wherever they happen
to find themselves.

Most of these games are ancient. It should be kept in mind
that before the end of the last century, most people in Europe,
as in the Americas, lived on farms and away from urban
centres. Rural children were largely isolated from contact with

others of their own ages. The farms were far apart from one another. Thus, the games that these children played among themselves were adaptable to wide age groups and were not dependent on given-sized teams or rigid rules. These same games are also ideal for present-day play streets in crowded cities, or for informal play when children casually meet in playgrounds and parks, and whenever they gather outside.

Hopscotch

Ages: 5 and older.
Number of players: 1 or more.
Equipment: A stick to scratch the diagram into soft ground, or chalk for pavement; a pebble, a small piece of wood or a shell as the counter that, in most English-speaking countries, is called the 'potsie.'
Place: Outdoors.

Countless versions of this game exist and are played around the world. Patricia Evans discovered at least 19 different ones played by children in San Francisco in 1955.[15] An ancient Hopscotch diagram has survived the centuries, inscribed in the pavement of the Forum in Rome. The game is known as *Marelles* in France, as *Tempelhüpfen* in Germany, and by the name of *Ekaria Dukaria* in India. Russian, Scandinavian, and Chinese children enjoy the same game played with minor variations.

The game of Home (see diagram) is played by throwing the 'potsie' into space number 1, jumping with the right foot into

8, hopping with the left foot into 2, with the right into 7, never keeping both feet on the ground until the first player has arrived at 'Home.' Here he can put both feet down. He returns, left foot into 5, right foot into 4, in turn, until he arrives at 1. Here he retrieves his 'potsie' while standing on one foot and then jumps out.

If the 'potsie' lands on a line, or when a player steps on a line, he is out and must start at his next turn as at first. But when a player completes the full round, he continues by throwing his 'potsie' into space number 2, completes a full round of hopping as before, jumps out, and then continues until he has thrown his 'potsie' into every space from 1 to 8, except 'Home,' hopping the full circuit each time. If he completes all rounds without fault, he closes his eyes and throws the 'potsie' aiming for 'Home.' If it lands inside without touching a line, he goes through the diagram once more, eyes closed, first stepping into 1 and 8 with both feet at the same time, next into 2 and 7, all the way to 'Home' and back again. If he completes this round without stepping on any lines, picking up his 'potsie' on 'Home' and finally jumping out, he has won that game and a new round begins.

Variation 1 (see diagram): The first player throws his 'potsie' into 1, hops with both feet into 1 and 2, respectively, then hops with one foot into 3, and continues, hopping alternately with two feet and with one until he reaches 12 and then returns, hopping in the same manner in the opposite direction. If he completes this round successfully without stepping on any

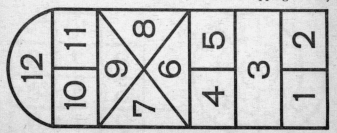

lines, this same player aims his 'potsie' at 2, hops all the way through the diagram once more as before, picking up his 'potsie' on his return trip, when he reaches the space into which it was thrown and so on, until he has thrown the 'potsie' into all the numbered spaces. That player wins who completes the whole round of throws and hops successfully. He loses his turn whenever his 'potsie' or a foot lands on a line.

Variation 2: The following diagrams show different Hopscotch diagrams used by children of the past and present, with and without numbers, played by hopping on a single foot, on both, or alternately on one and then on both. The rules are more or less similar to those described above.

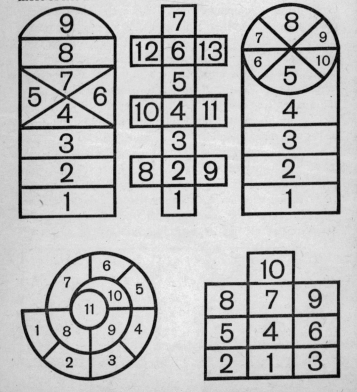

Variation 3: An old English version of this game requires each player to kick the 'potsie' from square to square as he hops into it, starting at 1, hopping up to 12 on one foot and back again to 1 and then out. On completing this round he goes through the next as before, carrying the 'potsie' on the back of his hand, next on his forehead, next bent over on the small of his back, then on the right shoulder, and finally on his left shoulder. If, on the first or on any succeeding round, he kicks the 'potsie' onto a line, or when, on succeeding rounds, he drops it or if he steps on a line, he is out and must await his next turn.

Rope-skipping
Ages: 6 and older.
Number of players: 1 or more.
Materials: Skipping-rope.
Place: Outdoors.

Rope-skipping by individual children and groups is sometimes accompanied by the singing of game rhymes, of which the following is typical. The rope is swung and the player skips, keeping the rhyme's beat:

'Mother, Mother, I am sick,
Call for the doctor, quick, quick, quick.
In came the doctor, in came the nurse,
In came the lady with the alligator purse.
Out went the doctor, out went the nurse,
Out went the lady with the alligator purse.'

Joseph Strutt, the early-nineteenth-century author of the book *Sports and Pastimes of the People of England*, describes rope-skipping as follows:

'This amusement is probably very ancient. It is performed by a rope held at both ends, that is, one end in each hand, and thrown forwards or backwards over the head and under the feet alternately. Boys often contend for superiority of skill in this game, and he who passes the rope about most times without interruption is the conqueror. In the hop season, a hop-stem stripped of its leaves is used instead of a rope, and in my opinion is preferable.'[32]

Variation 1: Two players turn the rope slowly at first, then faster, while a third skips until he (or she) trips or misses a skip. Then one of the others takes his place. Players keep score of the number of times each manages to skip successfully before tripping.

Variation 2: The two players who hold the rope ends swing it from side to side, instead of turning it in a complete circle as before. The third player skips – either with both feet together, or first with one foot and then with the other.

Variation 3: CHASE THE FOX: A game for 5 or more players. Two turn the rope. One of the other players is chosen the leader. The rest must follow and do exactly what the leader does in their turn. The following sequence is typical:

(a) The leader 'runs,' but does not skip, through the rope while it is up high. The rest follow in turn.

(b) The leader jumps into the turning rope, skips once, and then jumps out again. The rest follow.

(c) The leader jumps into the turning rope, skips twice . . . and so on.

The first player to trip on the rope takes the place of one of the rope-turners.

Variation 4: One player turns the rope and skips. A second player runs through the rope while it is up high and, facing the rope-turning player, skips with him once and runs out. Each of the other players follows in turn.

Variation 5: Two players turn the rope. A third runs in, carrying a stone or pebble. He places the stone on the ground and picks it up again at each alternate skip.

Variation 6: Two players turn two ropes at the same time in either the same or opposite directions. The other players, in turn, are required to skip both ropes.

Variation 7: One player turns and skips the rope himself (or two rope-turners swing it for a third). But the rope must pass twice beneath the skipper's feet at each leap.

Cock-fighting
Ages: 6 and older.
Number of players: 2 or more.
Place: Outdoors.

Each player stands on one foot and grasps his other by the ankle in one hand. Both players hop around and bump into each other, attempting to knock the opponent off balance. That player wins who forces his opponent off balance, to let go of his foot, or to place both feet on the ground.

This and the following games can be played by any number of participants, the winner of each round opposing the next player, or the winners of rounds opposing each other, or as a free-for-all.

Variation 1: Players hop on one foot, with arms folded across their chests.

Variation 2: Each of 2 opposing players squats on his haunches, putting his arms around his knees and clasping his hands firmly. Players hop as before, trying to unbalance one another.

Variation 3: Players squat as above. But they are required to face each other with toes touching, throughout the contest.

Variation 4: Draw a circle around each 2 opposing players. Without using the free hand (placing it behind their backs) in the first game cited above, or playing according to any of the other versions, that player wins who forces his opponent to touch or to cross the circle.

Leapfrog
Ages: 6 and older.
Number of players: 2 or more.
Place: Gym or outdoors.

Caution players not to make fists while leaping over another's back, to make 'firm' backs, and to stand rigid and still while others leap over them.

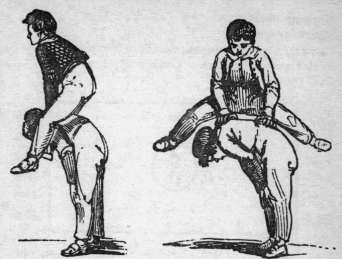

One player makes a 'back' by bending forward and down and by placing his hands on his knees to make a 'high back' or elbows on knees to make a 'small back' as demanded by each leaping player. The second player then leaps over the first and makes a 'back' in turn at about 1·5 metres (5 feet) distance from the first. The first player then leaps over him and so on. In a game of more than 2 players the first and second players remain in place until the third has jumped; all 3 then remain in place until the fourth has jumped and so on, until all players are making 'backs' at the same time. The last player in line, who leaped first, then straightens up, leaps over all others and makes a 'back' again at the head of the line. The game continues for as long as players agree.

Variation: Leapfrog can also be played as a race game. Players divide into two or more equal teams and commence, as before, on the word 'Start' from the referee. Players only leap over those of their own team. That team wins whose last player first completes jumping over all of his team-mates and stands first in line ahead of his team.

Hopping bases

Ages: 6 and older.
Number of players: 12 or more (must be an even number),
divided into two equal teams, plus one 'it' player.
Place: Outdoors.

A playing field is marked, 18 metres (60 feet) (or more) long
and 4·5 metres (15 feet) (or more) wide. A 90 cm (3-foot) circle
is marked in the centre for 'it' (see diagram).

'It' is chosen by lot. The members of each team line up on
opposing base lines of the field. 'It' stands in a circle in the
centre. At the command from 'it,' the members of both teams
start hopping on one leg, from one end of the field to the
other. 'It' may stand on both legs as long as he stays in his
'castle.' But in order to tag the hopping players, he must leave
his castle and hop like the rest. All tagged players, and any
player who puts his other foot down, are 'out,' with the exception of 'it.' If he puts his other foot down, he must return
and step inside his castle before venturing forth once more to
tag players. Any player who reaches the opposing base is
'safe.' The game ends when all players have reached opposite
base lines or have been captured by 'it.' Then a new 'it' is
chosen for the next game.

Variation 1: The same playing field is used, but without castle
or 'it' player. Two equal teams line up on the base lines on
opposing sides of the field and, on the word 'Go,' hop on one

foot towards the opposite side of the field. Opposing team members try to unbalance each other. Any player who loses his balance or puts his other foot down is considered captured by the opposing team and must go to the base line towards which that team hops. Any team member who has crossed the opposite base line is safe. But any captured player may be rescued by any member of his own team who hops up to him and touches him. The team wins which crosses the opposing base line with the greatest number of its members.

Any player may hop back to his starting boundary line to take a rest. Once he crosses the opposing line, he may not re-enter the game.

Variation 2: In another version of the latter game described above, players of each team merely sally forth to capture opponents, returning them to their original starting base. That team wins which captures the largest number of opponents.

Variation 3: All players line up at one end of the field and hop on either right or left foot (determined before the start of the game) towards the opposite finishing line. The player who crosses the line first is the winner. Any player who puts his other foot down during the race is out of the game.

Variation 4: One player is chosen to be 'it.' All players, including 'it,' grasp their own right feet with their right hands and hop. 'It' tries to tag another player in this manner. None of the players, including 'it,' may put both feet on the ground except when standing still. If 'it' has both feet on the ground while tagging a player, it doesn't count. If he puts his foot down or lets go of it while chasing a player, he is required to tag two players before he is released. Only the second tagged player changes places with him. 'It' may be required to tag more than two, depending on the number of times he is seen putting his other foot down, or releasing his hold on it, while chasing another player. Any other player is required to change places with 'it,' if 'it' sees him putting his other foot on the ground or releasing his hand hold on it while hopping.

Obstacle hop

Ages: 7 and older.　　　　　*Materials:* Stones (or pegs).
Number of players: 2 or more.　*Place:* Outdoors on soft ground.

The stones or pegs are placed to mark an obstacle course. Players must hop, on one leg, in and out of the stones or pegs in a given manner (see diagram) from start to finish. One player hops at a time. Each player is timed. The player who completes the course in the shortest time period is the winner. Any player who loses his balance while on the course, or whose other leg touches the ground, is out of the game.

Originally, blindfolded players were required to dance on one foot around a number of eggs laid out over a piece of ground, a dance floor, or a stage. Anyone who stepped on an egg was the loser. Such egg-hopping dances were common in the days of the English poet Chaucer (d. 1400), and were still in vogue during the reign of Queen Elizabeth I.

Jump up

Ages: 7 and older.
Number of players: 2 or more.
Materials: 2·5-metre (8-foot) string (or light rope), with a paper bag attached that contains a quantity of sand sufficient to allow the bag to be swung in a circle steadily (see illustration).
Place: Outdoors.

One player, chosen by lot, stands in the middle, holding the end of the rope. The other players stand in a circle around him, close enough so that, when the centre player swings the rope with the bag attached, they must hop to avoid it. Any player

who fails to jump in time, and whose legs become caught in the rope, is out of the game. The last player to remain in the game changes places with the player in the middle for the next round.

5
Race, Tag, and Catch Games

The Olympic Games, held for more than 1,000 years, from 776 B.C. to A.D. 394, in the valley of Olympia in Greece, originally featured just a single event – the 200-yard dash. The Roman emperor Theodosius banned these quatri-annual games because of bitter quarrels between his regime and that of the Greeks. The Olympics were not revived until 1896, and with the exception of the World War I and II years, have been held every four years since.

Men have run races from and with predators and each other, and for sport, since time immemorial. Children have raced on their way to and from school, and in fields and parks, on the beach and in gardens and playgrounds. They have also invented variations on this simple activity that, in most instances, requires nothing but rules and a pair of legs.

Running races
Ages: 4 and older.

Number of players: 2 or more.
Equipment: See individual variations.
Place: Outdoors or indoors.

The simplest form of running race merely requires that a starting line and a finishing line be marked at a distance, in a straight line or on a circular track. Players line up at the start and race at a given signal. The winner is the player who first crosses the finishing line at the end of the course, or after covering several laps.

Variation 1: EGG AND SPOON RACE

Equipment: 1 large spoon and 1 egg for each player.

Players race as above, except that each is required to hold an egg in a spoon in one hand, and carry it from start to finish. That player wins who first crosses the finishing line with his egg intact on the spoon. No player may use his other hand to hold or steady the egg. Any player is out of the game if he drops his egg or uses his other hand to steady either spoon or egg. This game may also be played as a relay game (see Relay Races, p. 126), or with table tennis balls or other small balls carried on spoons as substitutes for eggs.

Variation 2: SACK RACE

Equipment: 1 potato sack for each player; twine, sufficient to tie the sack at the waist of each player.

Each player steps into a sack, tying it around his waist. Players hop from start to finishing line. Any player who falls may get up and continue to hop. The player who crosses the finishing line first is the winner.

Stoop tag

Ages: 4 and older.
Number of players: 8 or more (up to about 12).
Place: Indoors or outdoors.

All players but one form a circle. The extra player stands in the centre. The players in the circle skip round and round, singing any song they know or reciting any common nursery rhyme.

As soon as they have finished, all must stoop (or sit) down.
The player in the centre tries to tag any player before he stoops
(or sits) down after each rhyme or song has ended. The tagged
player must then stand in the centre. The first centre player
joins the circle, and the game continues.

Musical chairs
Ages: 4 and older.
Number of players: 8 or more.
Equipment: Chairs – 1 less than the number of players; piano
(or radio or gramophone).
Place: Indoors.

Chairs are set up back-to-back in two more or less equal rows.
The players line up, forming a circle around the chairs. One
other person is required to play or to start and to stop the

music. At the start of the music, all players start walking or running around the island of chairs. Whenever the music stops, each player must try to sit in an empty chair. No two players may occupy the same chair. The player who is left standing is out of the game. Another chair is removed before the music begins again. At the resumption of the music, players get up and walk or run as before – and so on. The player who manages to sit in the last remaining chair wins the game.

Variation 1 – MUSICAL BUMPS: The same rules apply as before, except that the game is played without chairs. Place sheets or squares of paper in a row on the floor, one less than the number of players. When the music stops each player tries to find a square of paper on which to sit. The player left without paper is out of the game. Remove one additional square of paper before starting the music. Players continue to march or run around the line of paper squares, playing as at first. The last remaining player wins the game. The game may also be played without paper squares, in which case the last player to sit on the floor, when the music stops, is out.

Variation 2 – PASS THE PARCEL: Players form a circle, standing or sitting. A wrapped sweet is passed from one to the next while the music plays. That player who holds the sweet in hand at the moment when the music stops is out of the game. The last player to remain in the game is the winner and may eat the sweet. Alternatively, the sweet may be wrapped in numerous layers of paper. The player holding the parcel when the music stops attempts to unwrap it, but must pass it on when the music starts. The player who finally unwraps the sweet may eat it.

Oranges and lemons
Ages: 6 and older.
Number of players: 6 or more.
Place: Gym or outdoors.

Two players, chosen by lot, hold hands and form an arch with upraised arms. One of these two players chooses to be the 'lemon,' the other the 'orange,' by mutual agreement, but out of hearing of all other players. The rest line up and run through the arched arms in a continuous circle singing:

'Oranges and lemons
Say the bells of Saint Clements
I owe you five farthings
Say the bells of Saint Martins
When will you pay me
Say the bells of Old Bailey
When I grow rich
Say the bells of Shoreditch
When will that be?
Say the bells of Tralee
I do not know
Says the great bell of Bow
Here comes a candle to light you to bed
Here comes the chopper to chop off your head
Chop, Chop, Chop!'

On the words 'Chop, Chop, Chop' the first two players lower their arms and try to catch one of the running players. The caught player is asked in a whisper whether he chooses to be a 'lemon' or an 'orange.' On making his decision he lines up behind whichever of the first two players matches his or her choice. It is important that none of the other players know until the end of the game which each caught player chose. The game continues as before until all running players are caught and are lined up behind the 'lemon' and 'orange' player respectively. The game ends with a tug of war between both sides.

Follow my leader
Ages: 5 and older.

Number of players: 6 or more.
Place: Indoors or outdoors.

Players line up, one behind the other, without touching or holding one another. The first in line is chosen by lot. All others are required to follow him wherever he goes, doing exactly what he does and imitating his every gesture. If he hops, they hop, etc. Any player who fails to 'follow the leader' is out of the game. It is best to play each 'turn' of this game for a predetermined time period, at the end of which a new leader is chosen. Those players win who remain in line at the end of each round.

Variation: Players line up side by side, holding hands. The leader starts out as before. Whenever any player fails to 'follow the leader,' he changes places with the player next to him who is closer to the end of the line. If two players release hands, both players change places with the next two who are closer to the end of the line. Any player who reaches the end of the line is out of the game. The rest of the rules remain the same.

Hoop games

Ages: 5 and older.
Number of players: 1 or more.
Equipment: Hoop and stick.
Place: Outdoors.

The earliest hoop game was probably invented by children playing outside a cooper's shop in the Middle Ages, or perhaps even earlier. There they may have picked up one of the iron hoops with which coopers bound wooden slats to form barrels. Finding that the hoops could be controlled by wooden sticks, the children made up all sorts of racing games, one of which is described below. Children have played with hoops ever since, except for an interval between the early part of this century and the appearance of the hoola hoop in the nineteen-fifties. Typical of many children's pastimes, this simple toy –

no different from its predecessors, except that it was made of plastic tubing – was suddenly rediscovered and became a temporary fad.

Players line up in a row and race toward a given, pre-determined finishing line (and back, if the ground is restricted in length). Each drives and guides his hoop with his stick. Any player whose hoop falls to the ground is out of the game. The first player to cross the finishing line wins.

Variation 1: Hoop games can also be played as relay games (see Relay Races, p 126).

Variation 2: A course is set up, marked by a number of gates consisting of 2 stones placed close together, but far enough apart that a hoop can be driven between them. A finishing line is marked. Each player in turn must drive his hoop from one end of the course to the other, steering it through each gate. Any player who fails to clear a gate or who upsets his hoop before reaching the finishing line is out of the game.

Tag

Ages: 5 and older.
Number of players: 3 or more.
Place: Outdoors or gym.

One player is chosen 'it,' and tries to chase and tag any of the others. As soon as he tags another player, the tagged player becomes 'it,' and so on.

Variation 1: Same rules as above, except that when a player runs between 'it' and the player being chased, 'it' *must* chase the intercepting player.

Variation 2 – TOUCH TAG: In this game, players agree beforehand on a common material – wood, metal, or any other. Whenever a chased player touches the specified material, he is safe for the time being, until 'it' chases another player.

Variation 3 – CARRY TAG: requires an object that is passed from player to player. 'It' may only chase and tag a player who holds the object. The object must always be in sight when carried by one of the players.

Variation 4: The first 'it' tags another player, who becomes 'it,' as usual. When the new 'it' tags another player, he must at the same time hold his hand over the place on his body where the first 'it' tagged him. The newly tagged player must do the same, and so on.

Variation 5: Each group of 3 players forms a line, each player grasping the waist of the player in front of him. It is the object of 'it' to attach himself to the last player of any group of 3 players. If he succeeds in so doing, the first in line of that group becomes 'it.' Any player in a group of 3 who lets go of the person in front of him becomes 'it,' whether or not his group has been tagged.

Variation 6: One player is chosen to be 'it,' and another as the 'runner.' The remaining players form a circle, each holding hands with his neighbours. 'It' stands inside the circle and the 'runner' outside at the start of the game. On the word 'go' from the 'runner,' he himself runs round the circle, dodging in and out between players, while the 'it' player tries to tag him. The players in the circle must raise their arms or make

room for either to pass. But 'it' must follow the 'runner' precisely through the same openings in the circle and he must imitate exactly what the 'runner' does, jumping, rolling on the floor or ground, hopping on one leg, or whatever he chooses to do. When 'it' manages to tag the 'runner,' the latter joins the circle; the player who was 'it' in the former round becomes the 'runner' for the next, choosing any player in the circle to be 'it' for the next round.

Variation 7 – SHADOW TAG: an outdoor, sunny-day version, in which one player is selected to be 'it.' The rest scatter, but they must remain in sunny or well-lit places. 'It' tags any other player when, having chased him, he manages to step on his shadow. A tagged player becomes 'it' in turn.

Fox and rabbit

Ages: 5 and older.
Number of players: 10 or more.
Place: Indoors or outdoors.

Players divide into groups of four. One of the remaining players is chosen as 'it,' and the other as the 'spare rabbit.' Three of each group of four form a circle (the rabbit warren) by placing their hands on each other's shoulders. The fourth member of each group becomes a 'rabbit' and squats in the centre of the circle. 'It' is the 'fox' and he attempts to tag the 'spare rabbit,' who may run into any warren for safety. The fox may not follow him or reach inside. But that rabbit who is already inside the warren into which the 'spare rabbit' ran for safety must then leave it at once, to be chased by the fox. At no time may more than one rabbit remain in any warren. The players forming any circle must allow the 'spare rabbit' to enter whenever he chooses to do so. The rabbit who must then run away becomes the 'spare rabbit' and, though he may choose any other warren for safety in the same manner as the first, he may not return to his original warren at that turn. Any tagged rabbit changes places with the fox.

Potato race

Ages: 5 and older.
Number of players: 2 or more.
Equipment: Use 6 or more potatoes – the same number – for each player's line. Other objects, like pebbles or ping-pong balls, can be used in their stead; chalk or stick for marking lines; empty carton or wastepaper basket for each player or team. *Place:* Indoors or outdoors.

Mark a starting line and place one row of potatoes for each player at right angles to the starting line, each potato 1·2 to 1·5 metres (4 or 5 feet) from the next. Place the carton or waste-paper basket at the end of each line. All players line up at the starting line, one behind each row of potatoes. On the word 'go' from the referee, each runs forward, picks up the first potato only, runs to the basket, drops or throws it in, and then returns for the next potato, and so on. The player wins that round who first drops the last of his potatoes in the basket.

Variation: This game may also be played as a relay game. Divide the players into equal teams, each of which lines up behind its own line of potatoes. Every line must contain as many potatoes as the number of players on each team. The first player, having dropped his potato into the basket, returns and tags the next player in line. who runs forward to do the same, and so on. The team wins whose last player first drops the last potato into his own team's basket and who returns, tagging the first player of his team.

Pair race
Ages: 5 and older.
Number of players: 13 or more – it must be an odd number.
Place: Indoors or outdoors.

Players pair up, holding hands, and stand in line. The odd player, chosen by lot to be 'it,' stands aside. At his command, 'Last pair go,' the last pair in the row of players split up and run toward the head of the column on opposite sides, trying to avoid being tagged by 'it.'

If either member of the pair is tagged, 'it' and the tagged player make a pair at the head of the column. The other partner of the first pair then becomes 'it,' and the game continues as before. If 'it' fails to tag either member of a pair before they hold hands again at the head of the column, he must continue to be 'it' for the next turn, and so on.

Cat and mouse
Ages: 5 and older.
Number of players: 12 or more.
Place: Outdoors or gym.

All but 2 players form a circle. They may not hold hands. Of the remaining players, one is chosen 'cat,' and the other 'mouse.' The cat stands inside the circle, and the mouse remains outside. The object of the cat is to try to get outside the circle to 'tag' the mouse. It is the object of the players in the circle to try to prevent the cat's escape. The mouse may not ever enter the circle. The game ends when the mouse has been tagged, or if the cat is unable to escape the circle after a predetermined time period.

Butterfly hunt
Ages: 6 and older.
Number of players: Two teams of 12 or more each.
Place: Outdoors or gym.

One team is designated as butterflies, the other as hunters. The hunters try to capture the butterflies by encircling them and joining hands to close the net. Captured butterflies are out of the game for that turn. Hunters may repeatedly net as many butterflies as they can at one innings. At the end of the time period allowed for one innings, captured butterflies score for the capturing team. Teams change places alternately for succeeding innings. The winning team is the one which has scored the largest catch at the end of a given number of innings.

Lion and gazelles
Ages: 6 and older.
Number of players: 8 or more.
Place: Outdoors or gym.

One player is chosen as the lion, and a place is marked for his den. The rest of the players are gazelles, who have a marked safety zone, some distance from the lion's den, within which they cannot be captured. All the gazelles start walking towards the lion, approaching closer and closer. The lion may dash out of his den at any time to chase one of the gazelles, who then tries to run back to his safety zone. If a gazelle is tagged before he reaches safety, he is captured by the lion and remains in his den. If he reaches his safety zone before being tagged, the lion loses 1 point. The game is played for a given time period, or until all the gazelles are captured. The last gazelle to be captured then becomes the lion.

Blind man's buff
Ages: 6 and older.
Number of players: 8 or more.
Place: Indoors or outdoors.

All players but one form a circle, facing inwards. The extra player is blindfolded and placed in the centre. The rest of the players hold hands and skip in a circle. The 'blind man' may

call 'stop' at any time, on which signal the players in the circle must stand in place. The blind man then points in any direction. The player closest to the blind man's pointed finger must step into the circle and try to keep away from the blind man. If the blind man tags him, he must stand still while the blind man touches his face and tries to guess his name. (Alternative rule: The blind man may ask the tagged player any one question other than his name.) If the blind man is able to guess the player's name, he is released, and the tagged player takes his place. If the blind man fails to guess the player's name, the game continues as before, the tagged player returning to his place in the circle.

Race for the empty space

Ages: 6 and older.
Number of players: 12 or more.
Place: Outdoors or gym.

All players but one stand in a circle facing inwards. The remaining 'it' player runs outside the circle and tags any player. The tagged player and 'it' must then run around the circle in opposite directions until they meet. On meeting, they grasp hands and swing each other once around in a circle, and then continue to run as before. The first player to reach the space vacated by the tagged player is safe. Whichever player remains becomes 'it,' and play continues as at first.

Hand-hold tag

Ages: 6 and older.
Number of players: 6 or more.
Place: Outdoors or gym.

One player is selected as 'it.' The rest of the players scatter. 'It' tries to tag one of the others. Whenever he succeeds, he and the tagged player join hands, and they seek to tag any of the others. Each tagged player joins the 'it' line. The last remaining untagged player is the winner.

Handkerchief tag

Ages: 6 and older.
Number of players: 10 or more.
Place: Outdoors or gym.

All players but one form a circle, facing inwards. 'It,' chosen by lot, runs around the outside of the circle, carrying the handkerchief. He drops the handkerchief behind any player in the circle. That player must pick up the handkerchief and chase 'it,' trying to tag him before he can safely run to the vacant place in the circle. 'It' must run once around the circle before he may occupy the vacant place. If 'it' is tagged, the second player returns to his place in the circle and gives the handkerchief back to 'it.' 'It' must then drop the handkerchief behind another player, who chases him as before.

If 'it' runs to the vacant place without being tagged, the chasing player becomes 'it,' and so on. The game continues for a given time period.

Counting out catch

Ages: 6 and older.
Number of players: 10 or more.
Place: Outdoors or gym.

Players agree to a number, considerably greater than the number of players. They line up in a circle and start counting off, starting with any player chosen by lot. Counting off continues until the determined number is reached. The player who counts off that number is 'it.' All other players scatter. 'It' must catch or tag any other player before he is released from being 'it.' The players agree to a new number, count off, and continue to play as before.

Variation: This same game can also be played using the alphabet, one letter being chosen for each turn. The rest of the rules remain as before.

Man in the middle

Ages: 6 and older.

Number of players: 10 or more.
Equipment: Two sets of markers or tape to indicate end zones and mid-point.
Place: Outdoors or gym.

One player is chosen by lot to be the 'Man in the Middle.' The rest are divided into two more or less equal teams. End zones are marked 35 metres (40 yards) or so apart (less for younger players), and another marker is placed halfway between them. Markers or tape should also indicate side boundaries. The Man in the Middle stands at the midpoint, and the teams line up one each at the end zones.

At the word 'go' from the Man in the Middle, each team starts running toward the opposite end zone, keeping within boundaries. The Man in the Middle may also leave his place, and he tries to tag as many of both teams as he can before they cross their respective end zones. Each tagged player must go directly to the midpoint and await the end of that turn. When all players who were not tagged have returned to their end zones, the Man in the Middle returns to his starting point, and the game begins anew on his shout of 'go,' except that all tagged players now aid him in tagging team members as they cross from one end zone to the other. The last player to be tagged is the winner.

Variation 1: This game may be played in a closed street, the edges of the pavement being the end-zone boundaries. Or all players may line up on one side of the street (or field) and try to run to the opposite side at the command of the Man in the Middle.

Variation 2: Players are divided into three equal teams. Two teams line up on one side of the street or playground respectively. The third team lines up in the centre. The members of the third team must hold hands. All other players may run individually. On the word 'go,' the two teams on opposite sides of the street or playground try to cross over and change places. The team in the middle tries to tag as many players as possible while the others are crossing. Any tagged player is out of the game. The game ends after a given time period, or when all members of the two crossing teams are captured. Teams then change places, and one of the other two teams becomes the 'Team in the Middle.' The game should continue for at least three rounds, giving each team one turn in the middle. The team that captures the largest number of opponents wins.

This is a variation of a game called Barley Break, played for centuries by the children of England and Scotland.

Three's a crowd
Ages: 6 and older.
Number of players: 24 or more.
Place: Outdoors or gym.

All but two players stand in pairs, one player behind another, to form a double circle, facing inwards. The remaining two players, chosen by lot, are 'it,' who does the chasing, and the 'catch-me' player, who runs from him. Both players start from opposite sides of the circle and may run on either or both the inside or the outside of the circle in either direction, or may dodge between the players forming the double circle.

Whenever the 'catch-me' player feels himself threatened, he may stand directly behind any one of the couples that form the circle. When he does so, the front player of that couple becomes the 'catch-me' player and must run from 'it.' If 'it'

tags the 'catch-me' player before he stands safe, they change places. The game continues for a predetermined time period.
Variation 1: All but two players, chosen by lot, are divided into couples, each player facing and holding both hands with his partner. 'It' then chases the other extra player and tries to tag him. If the chased player ducks under the arms of any couple, he is safe in the 'cage' so formed. But the person whom the chased player faces must then release his hold and run from 'it' until he is either safe in a 'cage' or tagged. Any tagged player must chase 'it' in turn. Any 'caged' player takes the place of the person whom he faces. (See also Fox and Rabbits.)
Variation 2: Two players – one to be 'it' and the other to be the 'runner' – are chosen by lot. The remaining players pair off and each pair links arms. On the word 'Start' from the 'runner,' 'it' chases and tries to catch him. The runner may seek safety by linking arms with any couple, at which moment the member of that couple with whom he does not link arms must release his partner to become the 'runner' in turn. Any tagged player changes places with 'it,' who then becomes the 'runner.'

Number

Ages: 6 and older.
Number of players: 11 or more.
Equipment: Cards or sheets of paper, at least 15 × 22 cm (6 × 9 inches), marked with one number each, from 1 to a number one less than the number of players.
Place: Indoors.

One player is chosen to be 'it.' The rest sit in a circle, each holding one card, number side facing the centre of the circle. 'It' then calls out any two numbers shown on the cards. The 2 players holding these numbers must get up and try to change places without being tagged by 'it.' A player whose number has been called may not return to his original place, but must run or dodge, inside or outside the circle of players, until he gains the place of the other player or until he is tagged. 'It' changes places with a tagged player.

Variation: This game can be played without numbers, using the names of players, with letters of the alphabet marked on cards, or with numbers as above, for which 'it,' instead of calling out two marked numbers, must name them, each multiplied by two (or three or more, as agreed to before the start of the game). In other words, when 'it' calls 4 and 6, 2 and 3 must try to change places. (See also Number Games.)

Grandmother's footsteps

Ages: 6 or older.
Number of players: 4 or more.
Place: Indoors or outdoors; mark off two parallel lines, 6 to 22 metres (20 to 75 feet) apart.

One player, chosen to be 'it' by lot, stands on one line with his back to all others who are lined up toeing the other line. 'It' counts to ten as rapidly as possible. While he counts, the other players may advance as many paces as possible towards the line on which 'it' stands, by putting one foot directly in front of the other for each step. At the count of ten 'it' may turn around. The other players must then stand stock-still. If 'it' can catch any player moving or taking a step when he turns around, that player must then return to the starting line and the game resumes as before. The first player to cross the line on which 'it' stands changes places with him. Then 'it' joins the rest of the players and the game starts again as at first.

Three-legged race

Ages: 7 and older.
Number of players: 4 or any larger even number.
Equipment: Cloths, handkerchiefs, or twine.
Place: Outdoors or gym.

Players pair off. Each two players stand side by side and tie the right leg of one to the left leg of the other, using a cloth or twine. Make sure that legs are not tied tightly and circulation is not restricted. All players line up at a starting line and race towards a finishing line marked at a convenient distance. The first pair of players to cross the finishing line are the winners.

Count to one hundred or hide-and-seek

Ages: 7 and older.
Number of players: 6 or more.
Place: Outdoors.

One player is chosen as 'it.' He must remain near a tree or other goal, facing it with his eyes closed while he counts out loud to 100 (or any other number agreed upon). The other players hide. When 'it' reaches his last number, he opens his eyes, leaves the goal, and tries to find the other players. As soon as he spots another player, he must call out his name. Both then run toward the goal. If 'it' reaches the goal first, the second player becomes the 'spy.' If the second player reaches the goal first, he is safe, and 'it' must continue to find and race other hidden players.
Variation: Other simple hide-and-seek games for younger children can include indoor and outdoor hiding games without the 'race' feature of the above version.

Hand it over

Ages: 7 and older.
Number of players: Two teams of 12 or more each.
Place: Outdoors or gym.

Players are divided into two teams – cops and robbers. The robber team selects an object that can be carried in a pocket of one of the players without being visible to the opponents. The robber team lines up on one side of the play area and, on command, crosses over to the other side, running, walking, and dodging the opposing 'cop' team that is in the middle of the field. It is the object of the 'cops' to tag as many robbers as possible before they reach the other side of the playground.

The cops must demand, and a captured player who has it in his possession must give up, the hidden object. If one of the captured players has the hidden object, the cops win, teams change places, and the game resumes as before. If none of the captured robbers has the hidden object, the remaining robbers cross over once more as before. Captured players are out of the game for that turn.

Each crossing from one side to the other scores for the robber team. That team wins which has captured the robber holding the hidden object in the least number of cross-over runs, in the number of turns agreed on before the start of the game.

Relay races
Ages: 7 and older.
Number of players: Two or more teams of 6 or more players each.
Equipment: Stick (or cloth, ball, or bowling pin) for each team; markers for starting and goal lines.
Place: Outdoors or gym.

Each team lines up behind its own starting line. The first player is given the ball (or other object). On a given signal, each team's first player races toward the goal line, touches or crosses it, and returns to the front of his team's line. He passes the ball to the next player of his team, then goes to the end of the line. The second player runs to the goal line and back, and passes the ball to the third player, and so on. That team wins whose last player is first to return to his team's starting line with the ball. *Note:* The distance between starting and goal lines should be determined according to the ages and stamina of the players.

Variation 1: Instead of carrying an object, each player may merely slap the hand of the next player on his return to the starting line.

Variation 2: The goal line consists of a circle of skittles that the first player must knock down. The second runner must set them up again before he returns to his team; the third player knocks them down again, and so on.

Variation 3 – HURDLE RELAY: The first two players of each team hold a rope or stick between them, low enough so that any other player can jump over it. The rest of the players of each team line up 6 or 7 feet (about 2 metres) from the hurdle. Each player must jump the hurdle and then return to the end of the line. When all team members have jumped, the player first in line takes the place of one hurdle holder, who goes to the end of the line. The players in line then run and jump as before. After all team members have jumped once more, the new player first in line takes the place of the hurdle holder who has not yet jumped, and the game continues as before. The winner is the team whose last player is first to return to the end of the line, after all team members have both jumped the hurdle and taken a turn at holding it.

Variation 4: In any of the above relay games, players may be required to hop on one or two legs, instead of running. Or the relays may be run piggyback, the first player carrying the second, who, on returning to the starting line, carries the third, and so on.

Variation 5: Instead of carrying a ball, each team's first player is given a word, a sentence, a number, or a sequence of numbers to memorize. On returning to his team after running the course, he passes this message on to the next player, and so on. That team wins whose last runner is first to return to his team and recite the correct message.

Variation 6: Other stunts each relay racer may be required to perform can include: balancing a pencil in his palm while he runs or walks; taking off his shirt and putting it on again at the goal line before he returns to his team; taking off and putting on his shoes, and so on. Or each team member may be required to perform some physical stunt at the goal line before returning to his team – such as climbing a rope, turning a somersault, skipping a rope 6 times, etc.

Variation 7: At each turn, the last player in each team's line calls out an object that the front member of the opposite team must run to and touch before returning and tagging the next team member in line. The last player in line must call out the next objective for his opposing team's next runner before the first runner returns to his starting line.

Variation 8: Players divide into two equal teams. Each team's members sit in a row or circle of their own. On the word 'Start' from the referee, the first player of each team, chosen by lot, races all around his own team's row or circle of players and returns to his seat. As soon as he is seated, the next player gets up and completes the course, and so on, until all players of one team have run and are seated once more. That team wins whose last player to run first returns to his seat.

Green and blue
Ages: 7 and older.
Number of players: Two teams of 6 or more each; 1 referee.
Place: Outdoors or gym.

The referee is chosen by lot. The two teams, one called Green, the other Blue, line up 8 to 10 paces apart, with their backs to each other. A finishing line is marked 30 or more paces ahead of each line of players. The referee stands between teams.

The object of whichever team is called by name (Blue or Green) by the referee, is to race to the finishing line facing the opposing team – i.e., to the line behind the called team's backs. The other team tries to tag as many runners as possible before they reach the finishing line.

If the number of runners reaching the finishing line is greater than the number tagged, the running team wins. If the tagged number is greater, the pursuing team wins. Succeeding turns continue as at the start of the game.

Slap tag
Ages: 7 and older.
Number of players: Two teams of 6 or more players each.
Place: Outdoors or gym.

Each team lines up, with arms outstretched, behind a line 18 metres (20 yards) or more from the opposite team. One member of either team is selected to start running towards the opposing team. When he reaches the opposite side of the field, he slaps the hand of any player, and tries to run back and cross his own starting line. The slapped player chases him and tries to tag him. If the first player is tagged before he crosses his own starting line, he is captured and is out of the game. Whether or not the second player tags the first, he in turn slaps the hand of an opposing player, who chases him back to his own finish line. The game continues until all the members of one team are captured, or for a predetermined time period, at which time the team with the largest remaining number of players is the winner.

Send-off
Ages: 7 and older.
Number of players: Two teams of 6 or more players each.
Place: Outdoors or gym.

The two teams, one designated Green, the other Blue, line up separately in parallel lines. The first player of the Blue team stands 50 or so paces ahead, facing both lines. It is the object of the first player of the Green team to intercept and tag the first Blue team player before the latter can return and touch the last player in line on his own team. If the player is tagged, he changes teams and stands at the end of the Green team's line, playing in turn like the rest. If the first Green player fails to tag the first Blue player, he then changes teams and stands at the end of the Blue team's line.

On the following turn, a Green team player stands 50 or so paces ahead of both teams. Then it is the turn of the Blue team player next in line to try to tag him. The game continues either for a predetermined time period, or until one side has tagged and captured all players.

Prisoners' base
Ages: 7 and older.
Number of players: 10 or more players divided into even-numbered teams; 1 referee.
Place: Outdoors or gym.

Each team gathers in opposing fields. On the word 'Start' from the referee, members of each team try to cross into the opponents' field and to reach the 'prison' on that side. When any player enters or manages to touch or to put one foot into an opponent's prison, if he is not tagged before he does so, *and only if that prison is empty*, the innings ends with a score of 1 point for that player's side. The game then resumes as at first.

A player may be tagged and imprisoned by the tagging side while he is inside the opponents' field. All prisoners can be freed when a player of the same side as the prisoners' manages to reach that prison without being tagged and touches any one prisoner inside the prison. Prisoners may lean out of each

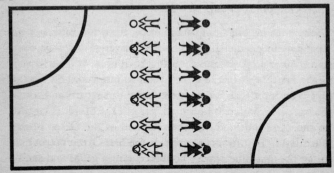

prison to be touched by a member of their own side, provided they keep at least one hand or foot inside the prison.

Released prisoners and the player who released them must return to their own side of the playing field, while all other players stand in place. All then continue to play as before. But at the end of each innings all players, except prisoners who are not released, must return to their respective sides.

The game continues for a given number of innings or for an agreed-upon time period. That team wins which scores the largest number of innings at the end of a game or has imprisoned all members of an opposing team.

Variation: Small sticks or pebbles are placed inside each team's prison. Whenever a player reaches the opposing team's prison, and if no prisoners are inside it, he may take one stick and try to return it to his own side without being tagged, placing it inside his own team's prison. If he is tagged before crossing into his team's territory, he loses the stick and he and it are returned to the prison of the team from which he took it. All other rules remain as before. That team wins which either succeeds in liberating all sticks from an opponents' prison or imprisons all opponents.

Poison

Ages: 7 and older.
Number of players: 12 or more.
Equipment: Chalk or stick to mark a circle.
Place: Outdoors or gym.

All players form a circle. A smaller circle is drawn or marked inside this circle, leaving about 1·2 metres (4 feet) between it and the circle of players. All players link arms and then try to force one another to step onto or into the inner circle. The first player to do so becomes 'it,' while the others shout 'poison' and run away. 'It' must tag any of the others to end that round, and the game resumes as before. All players agree on a 'safe' material before the start of the game – stone or wood – that, when any player stands on or touches it, provides a safe haven against being tagged by 'it.' No player may carry this material with him while he is running.

Variation 1: This game may also be played by placing bowling pins to form the inner circle. The object is then to force any

other player to knock down one or more pins. The first one to do so becomes 'it.' The game proceeds as before.

Variation 2: Either game can be played without the 'tag' ending. On stepping on or across the inner circle or on up-setting a bowling pin, that player is 'out' for that round. The circle of players then re-forms and the game proceeds as before. When the number of players is reduced so that no circle can be formed, those remaining hold hands and run round the inner circle as before. That player wins who succeeds in forcing his last remaining opponent to step onto or into the circle, or to upset a bowling pin.

About face
Ages: 7 and older.
Number of players: 11, 18, 27, or 38.
Place: Indoors or outdoors.

In a game of 11 players, all but 2 form a square formation in ranks of three (see diagram). In a game of 18, all but 2 form a

square in ranks of four, as before, and so on. The 2 remaining players toss up to decide who will be 'it' and who will be the 'runner.' The rest of the players hold hands, forming parallel lines in a single direction (see diagram). 'It' and the 'runner' start in different ranks. On the word 'Go' from the 'runner,' 'it' chases him up and down and around the ranks trying to tag him. But the 'runner' may, at any time before he is tagged, call 'About face,' at which time all players in the ranks are required to turn ninety degrees in either direction to hold hands with their new partners to the right and left (see diagram). This regrouping of ranks can prevent the 'runner' from being tagged. When the 'runner' is tagged, he and 'it' choose 2 others from the ranks to take their places and they in turn join the rest. The game continues until all players have taken turns at being either 'it' or 'runner.'

Variation: The 'runner' may be required to call either 'Right turn' or 'Left turn,' so that all players in the ranks face in the same direction at all times.

Indoor tag

Ages: 7 and older.
Number of players: 8 or more.
Equipment: Chairs or pillows for all but 2 players.
Place: Indoors.

Clear all furniture from the room, except chairs (or pillows), sufficient for all but 2 players. Line up chairs or pillows in two or more equal rows, leaving ample space between the rows and between rows and walls. One player is chosen by lot to be 'it' and another to be the 'runner.' The rest sit down on the chairs or pillows, all facing in one direction, being sure to keep

their feet out of the rows to their left and right, keeping parallel aisles in one direction unobstructed. 'It' stands in the centre in front of the seated players. The 'runner' stands in the centre behind them. On the word 'Go' from the runner, 'it' chases and tries to tag him. Both may only run up and down the open aisles and around the front and back of the seated players, but never across the rows. When tagged, the 'runner' changes places with 'it.'

The 'runner' may seek safety by standing behind any of the rows of seated players, shouting 'Safe.' 'It' must then stand still until the foremost player in that row has got up from his seat and all players in that row have moved up one seat, giving the former 'runner' the opportunity to sit in the last and vacated chair in the row. The game then continues as before, 'it' being able to chase the new 'runner,' as soon as all players are seated again. The game is played for a time period agreed to before the start.

Hunt the fox
Ages: 7 and older.
Number of players: 10 or any larger even number of players; 1 referee.
Equipment: Chalk.
Place: Outdoors or gym.

Mark a double circle divided by as many diameters as half the number of players minus 2 (see diagram). One player, chosen by lot to be the hunter, stands in the centre. The rest are foxes who, all but one, stand, each to one den, where the diameters meet the outer circle. The remaining fox, chosen by lot, has no den and stands anywhere on the outer circle.

On the word 'Start' from the referee, each fox must leave his own den and run to any other along any of the marked lines. He may not run to either den directly to the left or to the right of his first one. The odd fox may run along any line to any den. At the same time the hunter leaves the centre and attempts to tag any fox who has not yet found a den. The hunter may only run along the paths. Once a fox or the hunter has started along a path, neither may turn back. But either can change direction whenever he comes to an intersection of paths. The first tagged fox changes places with the hunter and the game resumes as at first. When the hunter is unable to tag any fox before all but one have found a den, the referee declares a new 'start' and all foxes must exchange dens once more.

Circle-go-round
Ages: 7 and older.
Number of players: 12 or more; 1 referee.

Equipment: Chalk or stick.
Place: Outdoors or gym.

Draw or mark a large circle, 6 metres (20 feet) or more in diameter. Players form around the circle, each facing the back of the one in front of him. On 'Start' from the referee, all run round the circle. Each player tries to overtake the one in front of him, passing him on the outside and tagging him while he passes. Any tagged player is out of the race. That player wins who overtakes and tags the last but one player.

Variation: The referee may say: 'Turn about' at any point of the game, requiring all runners to run in the opposite direction. He may do so as often as he chooses during the game.

Wheelbarrow race
Ages: 7 and older.
Number of players: 4 or more.
Place: Indoors on a rug or outdoors on soft ground.

Mark a starting and finishing line 4·5 metres (15 feet) or more apart. Players pair off and line up behind 'start.' Each pair decides who shall play the part of the wheelbarrow first. The wheelbarrow player gets down on his hands and knees. The second player of each team picks up his partner's feet and, on the word 'Start' from the referee, guides his wheelbarrow toward the finishing line. The 'wheelbarrow' must walk all the way on his hands only. On arriving at the finishing line, the players of each team change places, he who first wheeled the wheelbarrow becoming the wheelbarrow in turn. Each pair then returns to start as before, as quickly as possible. That pair wins the game which first crosses the starting line.

Hare and hounds
Ages: 9 and older.
Number of players: 6 or more.

Equipment: A bag of scraps of coloured paper (or a piece of chalk).

Place: Outdoors – must be in a park or other large area.

One player is chosen as Hare and is given the scraps of paper or the chalk. He is given a start of 5 minutes, after which the other players may follow. The Hare must mark his course after every 100 steps, by making an agreed-upon mark with the chalk or by dropping a piece of coloured paper where it can be seen. He may double back or otherwise try to deceive his pursuers. The Hound who manages to track down the Hare and tag him is the winner.

6
Word Games

Many children have a difficult time learning to read because no one ever taught them to play with words. Certainly such play makes the use of words more appealing at early ages. Besides being fun, it helps children enlarge their vocabularies. At the very least, it stimulates them and gives parents and teachers one additional means of encouraging learning.

Word games, used at home and in school, can relieve the monotony of repetition and be substitutes for rote learning. They can dramatize a lesson or punctuate it so that children feel that learning is not exclusively serious; it can also be amusing.

Some of these games need nothing other than a lively imagination. They can be played in a car, on the beach, at the dinner table, or any place away from home where no materials are available. Others require paper and pencils, and can be fun for children of different ages at a party or at school. They can be converted into blackboard games in a classroom, for which the teacher is both the stimulator and the referee.

Consider, for the moment, that babies learn to speak by literally playing with sounds. By imitating them, by playing repetitive games like pat-a-cake or 'This little pig went to market,' by crooning, talking, and singing to them, a parent encourages early speech. And, when properly stimulated, children learn at an amazing rate. This simple method of learning through play is often forgotten once a child reaches the ages at which formal education begins – today, as early as nursery school or kindergarten. And while a certain amount of drill is essential to some aspects of learning, it is more important that the child is able to apply whatever he learns. Word games dramatize the benefits of a large and varied vocabulary. Those games that allow teaching of fact or principle can be arranged so that the child is not numbed by repetition.

Finally, word games can show children that play does not require 'things' or toys. For the most part, play depends on the child's own ingenuity and his knowledge of game and play lore. Man's fascination with words, with riddles and conundrums antedates the Oracle at Delphi. And play with words and ideas is an exclusively human preoccupation. So if you want your child to express himself and to play with words and ideas, he'll need to be shown some of the simple and traditional ways in which children and adults have used language in games.

Many of these word games can help children learn to observe, classify, and order their experiences. Others can teach them to follow directions or how to give them. At the very least, these games can awaken a consciousness that orderly and systematic methods of thought and action can lead to gratifying success by the shortest route.

These games and their rules, like all others, require adaptation to the abilities, development, and experience of individual children or groups. They can unlock and unfold a child's

ability to express himself imaginatively. Such games can enable him to convert into active play what he sees and hears around him, what was read to him and what he has been shown, in real life, at home, at school, on outings, and on TV.

Obviously, game-learning should not be the exclusive method employed, nor does all learning lend itself to translation into games. But certainly some aspects of learning can be eased and made more attractive, and can be combined with the teaching of social skills and self-expression.

Who am I ?

Ages: 4 and older.
Number of players: 6 or more.
Place: Indoors or outdoors.

One player is chosen by lot to be 'it.' He is blindfolded, or turned away from the rest against a wall or a tree. The referee points to any one other player who must then say at once: 'Peter Piper picked a peck of pickled peppers' (or some other agreed-to phrase or nursery rhyme). 'It' must then try to identify that player by name, without seeing him. If he succeeds, he changes places with that player. If he fails, the game continues as at first, with the referee choosing another player to be identified, until 'it' guesses a player's identity.

Variation: The blindfolded player stands in the centre of a circle made by the other players, who dance or run around him. They must stop and stand still when the blindfolded player commands them to do so. The blindfolded player then points in any direction with his finger. That player at whom he points must then leave the circle to stand about 30 cm (1 foot) in front of the blindfolded player, who asks him to make a noise like a given animal – to bark like a dog, to moo like a cow, or to meow like a cat. The blindfolded player must then guess that player's identity. If he succeeds, he changes places with that player. If he fails, the player returns to the circle and the game resumes as at first.

Cooperative tale
Ages: 4 and older.
Number of players: 2 or more.
Place: Indoors or outdoors.

One player – or an adult – starts a story by telling a few sentences, e.g., 'Once upon a time I went to the Zoo . . .' Each following player, in turn, adds whatever he wishes to the last player's sentence, e.g., 'The keeper had left a cage door open . . .' 'And so, just as I got there, a bear walked out . . .' and so on.

Nursery rhyme bee
Ages: 5 and older.
Number of players: 2 or mcre.
Place: Indoors or outdoors.

The first player recites the first line of any nursery rhyme. Each following player, in turn, recites the next line, or portion of a line, until the whole nursery rhyme is completed. The following player starts with the first line of any other such poem, and so on. It is best not to keep scores or to pit preschool children against one another competitively in this kind of game.

Bird, insect, or fish
Ages: 5 and older.
Number of players: 2 or more.
Place: Indoors or outdoors.

Each player chooses one category – bird, insect, or fish – at every turn. The next player is required to name one species of that category. For example, if the first player says, 'Fish,' the second might reply, 'Catfish.' If the second player gives a correct answer, he then demands that the third player name any species of a category that he chooses, and so on. Any player who fails to name a species of a requested category or who gives an incorrect answer, may not, at that turn, ask the next player to name an animal. Or play may continue without penalty, after discussion of any wrong choice.

If children are too inexperienced to play this version, simpler classifications can be chosen, like 'four-legged animals, two-legged animals, and animals that swim' or 'things with wheels and things that walk.' The object of the game is less to inform than to encourage children to classify what they know.

Variation 1: Each player is assigned an animal sound that he can identify and imitate, or a single child can represent a number of animals. Then tell a story, weaving in all the animals the child or the children have been taught to imitate, mentioning each as often as possible. Whenever such an animal is mentioned, the child is required to make the appropriate noises.

Variation 2: Players form a circle or decide on a given order of play. The first player makes an animal noise. The next player must guess it. If he guesses incorrectly, he loses his turn.

If he guesses correctly, he in turn makes an animal noise that the next player must identify, and so on. Any player who wishes may make a nonsense noise or other noise that is not made by an animal. If the next player says, 'Nonsense,' he continues in turn. But he loses his turn if he either fails to guess it, or identifies this noise incorrectly as one made by an actual animal.

Variation 3: The same game may also be played using transportation noises, sounds of the city, or sounds of the country. All rules of *Game Variation 2,* above, remain as before.

Because

Ages: 5 and older.
Number of players: 2 or more.
Place: Indoors or outdoors.

The first player describes any event in the simplest way, e.g., 'The toast burned.' The second player is required to give a reason, e.g., 'Because the toaster was turned up too high.' The third player (or the first, in a game of 2) must then state a probable effect – 'And everyone had charcoal for breakfast.' The next player starts with a new statement, and so on.

Players should be encouraged to state cause or effect as rapidly as possible. Any answer can be challenged by other players and must be defensible.

The ABC game

Ages: 5 and older.
Number of players: 2 or more.
Place: Indoors or outdoors.

The first player is chosen by lot. He names any letter of the alphabet. Each of the other players in turn must name, within 15 seconds (or any other agreed-to time period), a word that begins with that letter. Any player who fails to do so is out of the game. Once each child has taken his turn, the next player (chosen by lot or by agreement among players) names any other letter of the alphabet, and so on. No player may use a previously mentioned word. The last remaining player is the winner.

Variation 1: This game can be limited to cities, countries, nouns, verbs, flowers, animals, or any subject with which the children are familiar.

Variation 2: 'It,' chosen by lot, thinks of any object that is in sight and names its colour only. Each player in turn then tries to guess what it is. That player who first names the correct object becomes 'it,' chooses another object, names its colour, and asks the rest to guess what it is, and so on.

Variation 3: This game can be played by requiring 'it' to name the first letter of the name of any object that is in sight. The game is played as above.

Variation 4: These are simple games that can be adapted to use on car journeys and by older players, using objects that the car passes while the game is played.

Simon says (also known as O'Grady says)

Ages: 5 and older.
Number of players: 3 or more.
Place: Indoors or outdoors.

One player is chosen 'it' and becomes 'Simon'. The rest of the players either line up opposite him or form a circle around him. 'Simon' then performs gestures and describes them. *Example:* He touches his left ear with his right hand. He then says: 'Simon says: "Touch your left ear with your right hand." ' The other players must do exactly what he says and does. But, interspersed with describing what he does, 'Simon' may also say one thing and do another. When this happens, the players are always required to do what he says, but not what he does. For example, if he says: 'Simon says: "Touch your left ear with your right hand," ' but he touches his toes instead, the other players must touch their left ears with their right hands. Any player who touches his toes instead is out of the game.

'Simon' may also omit the 'Simon says' from the beginning of an instruction, for example he may say 'Touch your toes'. Any player who obeys such an instruction is out. When all players but one are out of the game, the remaining player changes places with 'Simon,' and the rest of the players re-enter the game and the game resumes as at first.

Variation: Players sit in a circle. The first is given a pencil or a spoon. He holds or taps it in any way he chooses, saying: 'Anyone can do that.' He then passes the spoon to the next player. That player must copy what the first player did, and then do something else with the spoon, saying to the next player: 'Anyone can do that,' and so on. Any player who fails to do exactly what the player before him did, is out of the game for that round.

I spy

Ages: 6 and older.
Number of players: 2 or more.
Place: Indoors or in a car.

One player, chosen by lot, decides on any person, animal or object that is in plain view of all others, without letting them know who or what was selected. He then announces: 'I spy with my little eye something beginning with A,' or with whatever letter of the alphabet his, her, or the object's name begins. All other players guess who or what it might be. Each player is allowed one guess per turn. The player who first guesses correctly becomes the next to ask the question.

All birds fly

Ages: 6 and older.
Number of players: 6 or more.
Place: Indoors or outdoors.

Each player, starting with one chosen by lot to be 'it' first, is given 10 turns to say: 'All birds fly.' He then names either a bird or any other animal or object and, flapping his arms while he speaks, says, for example: 'Eagles fly,' or 'Tables fly,' and so on.

Whenever he names an actual bird, all other players must flap their arms. But the object is to catch others unaware, so that they flap their arms even when the first player says: 'Elephants fly.' The naming player should vary actual birds with other animals or objects in a random order.

Any player who flaps his wings when anything other than a bird is named is out of the game for the remainder of that 'it' player's 10 turns. He re-enters the game when it is the next player's turn to be 'it.' That player wins who is able to make the largest number of players drop out during his 10 turns as 'it.' Airplanes, and people, objects, or animals that can be transported by plane, do not count as 'birds.'

Variation: The identical game can be played, with each player saying: 'All fish swim,' and then naming either a fish or a swimming mammal, saying, 'Whales swim,' or mentioning some other object or animal that cannot swim, while he flaps his arms. The rest of the rules remain the same. Ships, and people, objects, or animals that can be transported by ship, do not count as 'fish.'

How many words ?
Ages: 6 and older.
Number of players: 6 or more.
Place: Indoors or outdoors.

One player is selected to be 'it,' and another as timekeeper. 'It' leaves the room, while all other players, including the time-keeper, decide on any letter of the alphabet. 'It' is then invited back into the room and is told which letter was selected. While the timekeeper counts to 30, or to any other number agreed to before the start of the game, 'it' must recite as many words as he can think of that begin with the given letter. He must stop when the timekeeper stops counting. The number of words he was able to recite that begin with the given letter are his score for that turn.

Another is chosen to be 'it,' and the game continues as before, until all players have been 'it' in turn. That player wins who has the highest score at the end of the game.

The eating and drinking game
Ages: 6 and older.
Number of players: 2 or more.
Place: Indoors or outdoors.

Players sit in a circle or decide on a given order of play. The first player, chosen by lot, tells the next what he wants to eat or drink. *Example:* 'I want to eat an egg.' The next player must state where the food or drink originated: 'A hen [or a chicken] laid it.' He then goes on to tell the next player what he would like to eat, and so on.

Any player who cannot name the origin of the food or drink, loses that turn, may not tell the next player what he wants to eat or drink, and scores 1 point. That player wins who, at the end of a given number of turns, or at the end of a predetermined time period, has the fewest points.

Variation 1: This game can be played by allowing each player to state that he wants a given object. The following player is required, as before, to name that object's origin.

Variation 2: The object of each player is to ask a question that requires a Yes or No answer from the next. If the next player cannot answer or fails to answer correctly, he loses a turn and 1 point. The rest of the rules remain the same. It is the object of each player to ask his question in such a way that the next has difficulty answering him, or to ask a nonsense question that sounds as if it made sense.

Variation 3: Every player in turn may ask each of the other players one or more different questions in his turn. Anyone who uses the words Yes or No in his answer loses 1 point. That player wins who, after all have had their turn at asking questions, has the least number of points.

What is my job?
Ages: 6 and older.
Number of players: 2 or more.
Place: Indoors or outdoors.

The first player describes a job, naming only tools and an end-product, without defining the occupation itself, e.g., 'I use a hammer and a saw and I make tables. What is my job?' The second player must then define that occupation by title, e.g., 'A carpenter.' If he answers correctly, he asks the next player (in a game of more than 2 players) or the first (in a game of 2) to name an occupation that he describes in the same manner as the first player did. The game continues in turn. Any player who fails to give a proper definition, or one who asks the question in an unanswerable fashion, loses his turn.
Variation: Players may be asked, at their turn, to act out an occupation in pantomime. All other rules remain as in the game described above.

Take a trip
Ages: 7 and older.
Number of players: 2 or more.
Equipment: Blackboard and chalk; paper and pencil for each player.
Place: Indoors.

The teacher, or a player chosen by lot, writes a story on the blackboard, leaving out all nouns, leaving empty spaces in their place, and marking each space with a number.
Example:

1   went to   2   in order to find a   3   ! When he came to   4   , he went into the   5   and spoke to a   6   ! ... and so on.

Each child either draws a picture or writes down a noun. He numbers it according to the space into which it is supposed to fit. At the end of an agreed-to time period, each player reads the whole story or sentence, including the nouns he has drawn or written, each placed into its proper space.

Alphabet questions

Ages: 7 and older.
Number of players: 2 or more.
Place: Indoors or outdoors.

Players sit in a circle or decide on a given order of play. The first player, chosen by lot, asks the next in line a question about any object, animal, plant, person, or place, the name of which begins with the letter 'A.' *Example:* 'If I lived in America, what would I want to be?' The next player in turn must answer him with a sentence that makes sense and has an answering word (noun or adjective) beginning with the same letter. *Sample Answer:* 'I'd want to be an Astronaut.'

If the second player answers correctly, he may then ask the next player any other question, the noun of which begins with the letter 'B.' *Example:* 'If I were a Bat, what would I be?' The next player must answer as before, except that this time, the noun or adjective must begin with the letter 'B.' *Sample Answer:* 'I'd be Blind in daylight.' Play continues thus in turn until the whole alphabet has been completed.

Any player who fails to answer a question as required within a given time period, or who answers incorrectly, loses his turn to ask the next question and scores 1 point. That player wins who at the end of the game has the least number of points.

Question and answer

Ages: 7 and older.
Number of players: 2 or more.
Place: Indoors or outdoors.

The first 'it' is chosen by lot. He chooses any animal, occupation, object, or place (e.g., horse, carpenter, house, or farm) and asks each of the other players in turn one question in connexion with his chosen subject. All of his questions must be asked so that they can be answered with *Yes* or *No* or *Sometimes*. If a player answers '*No*,' he must be prepared to give the right explanation. *Example:* If 'it' has chosen horses, he may ask the next player: 'Do horses live in the country?' *Answer:* 'Sometimes.' 'It' then asks the third player: 'Do horses eat meat?' *Answer:* 'No, they eat grass, hay, oats, etc.' It is, of course, the object of 'it' to try to trip up his opponents.

Any player who gives the wrong answer is out of the game for that innings. Questions continue until only one of the other players is left. He then becomes 'it' in turn, and the other players re-enter the game.

Observation
Ages: 7 and older.
Number of players: 2 or more.
Equipment: Paper and pencil for each player; a number of small, common objects.
Place: Indoors.

All players remain outside the classroom or living room. Meanwhile, one player chosen by lot, or the teacher, places a number of objects on a table inside the room. The number and variety of the objects to be arranged depend on the ages and experience of the players.

Each player then returns to the room alone, and stays in it for an agreed length of time, looking at the heaped objects on the table. He then leaves the room, and once outside, writes down all the objects that he saw and can remember. The player or players win who can accurately remember, name, and describe one or more qualities of each object that was heaped on the table. For very young players, it is sufficient that each remember the objects only. Older players may be required to try to remember each object's colour, etc.
Variation: Instead of requiring players to leave the room, the designated first player or teacher may place the objects in a large paper bag. This bag is passed around the room or class.

Each player is then required to reach into the bag, but may not look into it. He may feel the objects in the bag for 20 seconds, and then must pass it on to the next player. When all players have had their turns, each then either recites or writes down the objects that he can identify and remember.

To avoid disputes among players, they may agree to be blindfolded in turn for playing the 'paper bag' variation of this game. When the game is used as a classroom game for pre-school children, objects in the bag may teach qualitative differences and similarities. For example: 'Describe the shape or texture of the objects and guess what each might be' . . . etc.

The shopping game
Ages: 7 and older.
Number of players: 2 or more.
Place: Indoors or outdoors.

The first player, and each in turn, tells the next: 'I am a . . . ,' and chooses the name of a storekeeper (or craftsman or professional), and then adds: '. . . and I sell . . . ,' naming any letter of the alphabet. Example: 'I am a baker and I sell [or make] C . . .' The next player must then guess all the things he makes, sells, or does, that begin with that letter. Possibilities for 'C' include: Cakes, Chocolate icing, Cheesecake, Cream puffs, Cottage loaf, Cupcakes and Coffee éclairs.

The second player – when he is unable to think of more such products that begin with the named letter, or when he makes a mistake by naming something that is not sold or made by a baker (or whatever merchant is named), or at the end of an agreed-to time – scores himself according to the number of correct things he has named. He then continues, like the first player, saying to the next: 'I am a . . . , and I make [or sell or do] G . . . [or any other letter of the alphabet that he cares to name].' The game continues until all players have had their turns. The player with the highest score wins.

Variation 1: This game may be played as a geography game,

with one player saying: 'I am from Africa [or any other continent, country or city] and I have B . . . [or any other letter of the alphabet],' and the next player then naming all the things he can think of that live, grow, or are found in that continent, country, or place that begin with the named letter. The game is played as before.

Variation 2: This game can be played as a transportation game. Each player in turn says: 'I am going to Australia [or any other country or town], and I am going by C . . . [or any other letter of the alphabet].' The game is played as before. But the manner of transportation named by the next player must be possible under the circumstances. In the given example, it would have to be 'Cargo plane,' 'Catboat,' 'Clipper ship,' 'Canoe,' or any other mode of transportation beginning with the letter 'C' that allows the player to cross the ocean. 'Car' would not be allowed.

Note: In any of these games, other players may challenge the player who names the letter to be used. If that player is unable to cite at least one example, he loses his turn.

Pantomimes

Ages: 7 and older.
Number of players: 3 or more.
Place: Indoors or outdoors.

Pantomimes are direct descendants from the Mime Plays of the Middle Ages, religious plays without words enacted in Europe's cathedrals. These in turn were derived from pagan rituals that predate historical times. They have been popular, and still are, in all cultures. Traditional Chinese and Japanese dramas are still acted out in silence, or at least without speech on the part of the players. There are, of course, any number of variations of pantomime games for individual children or groups. It would be futile to try to enumerate all of them.

As a teaching and learning device, and for party fun at home and in school, pantomimes allow children to act out what they know, to recall gestures, actions, detail, and processes, to help them move gracefully, and to recreate dramatically the sum of their experience.

The first player is chosen by lot and stands before the rest, acting out by gesture and sound effect, but without speech, an animal, a mode of transportation, a trade, a profession, or, in the case of older players, a chain of events. The other players must guess who he is, what he represents, or what story or event he is describing. The first player to guess what the pantomime represents becomes the next pantomime actor, and so on.

Variation 1: With children above the age of 8, several (3 or 4) players may be chosen to act out a pantomime for the rest. The players leave the room, agree to what they wish to represent, and try out their act out of sight of the rest. They then return to the room and enact their play without words. Sound effects are allowed. The first player who succeeds in guessing what the players represent may then choose 2 (or 3) others who have not yet had their turn as players, to create a new pantomime, as before. Play continues until all have had their turns.

Variation 2 – CHARADES: The same rules apply as before, except that each person or group acts out or mimes successive syllables of a chosen word. The other players must guess the whole word from the clues provided by the syllables. Any player who thinks that he can guess the word may do so, even before the whole word has been acted out. If he guesses incorrectly he is out of the game for that round.

Examples:

Type+writer.

Pa (father)+no!+ra (Egyptian god)+ma (mother)=
Panorama.

Words may be broken up into different parts that are not real syllables. They may also be represented so that they can only be recognized and understood phonetically:

Puree (mashed vegetable)+fire=Purifier.
Con (cheat)+struck+shun=Construction.

Forbidden words
Ages: 7 and older.
Number of players: 2 or more.
Place: Indoors or outdoors.

One player is chosen to be 'it' and leaves the room or stays out of earshot of the other players. The rest agree on a 'forbidden word.' When 'it' is recalled, all others engage him in conversation and ask him questions designed to make him use the 'forbidden word' as often as possible during an agreed-to time period. One player keeps score as to the number of times 'it' uses the 'forbidden word.' But none let 'it' know what word was chosen until the end of his turn.

The object of 'it' is to try to discover the 'forbidden word' and to avoid saying it. If he decides that he knows which word was chosen, and if he names the correct word during his turn, that turn ends and 'it' joins the rest of the players for another round. Another player is then chosen, until all have had their turn to be 'it.'

Each mention of the 'forbidden word' scores as 1 point against 'it.' But if 'it' guesses the word before the end of his turn, his total score is erased. At the end of a complete round, those players who have no score are given additional turns until only one player remains who has no score. He wins that game.

Variation: Each player writes six words on six different pieces of paper, keeping each, face down, in front of himself on the table. Each player, in turn, then asks every other player one question at one turn (or six questions of his opponent in a game of 2 players).

The object of each player, in asking his questions, is to try to induce his opponents to use one of the 'forbidden words' he wrote down on his slips of paper. Whenever an opponent uses a 'forbidden word' in answering, the questioning player turns up the slip on which that word is written and keeps it in full view on the table. That player wins who first turns up all six slips of paper.

Definitions
Ages: 7 and older.
Number of players: 2 or more.
Place: Indoors or outdoors.

The first player, chosen by lot, names any one object, place, animal, or shape, or anything else that occurs to him. The next player then must give a definition of the named object. For example, if the first player says, 'Cow,' the next must identify it in an appropriate manner, e.g., 'A domestic animal,' 'Bovine,' 'Cloven-hooved.' It is useful to have a dictionary or an encyclopedia at hand while playing this game.

Any player who fails to give a proper definition loses his turn to name an object for the next player.

The unfinished story game
Ages: 7 and older.
Number of players: 2 or more.
Place: Indoors or outdoors.

The first player tells a story involving a critical situation – a house is on fire, a car crashes, or two people climb a mountain and one falls into a ravine and is injured. The next player, and all others in turn, are required to provide a plausible ending to the story.

Rumour (or Pass the message)
Ages: 7 and older.
Number of players: 6 or more.
Place: Indoors or outdoors.

Players are seated in a circle. The first, chosen by lot, whispers a short sentence in the ear of the second. The second player repeats what he heard, or what he thinks he heard, by whispering this into the ear of the third, and so on, until the message reaches the last player. He then repeats the message as he received it and compares it to the sentence that the first player announces as the one that he whispered to the second player.

Which ant?
Ages: 7 and older.
Number of players: 2 or more.
Place: Indoors or outdoors.

Players decide on a syllable or word ending, like '-*ant*,' that is common for many different nouns. Others are suggested below. The first player then asks the second a question that provides a clue as to what he is talking about. *Example:* *Q:* 'Which 'ant' has a long nose and big, floppy ears?' *A:* 'An eleph-*ant*.' *Q:* 'Which 'ant' has leaves?' *A:* 'A pl-*ant*.'

In a game of 2 players, the first questions the second until he is stumped and cannot answer. It is then his turn to question the first, using the same syllable. In a game of more than 2 players, each asks the next one question in turn. That player wins who has given the largest number of correct answers at the end of a given number of turns.

Other syllables and word endings that can be used to play this game include -*ist*-, -*are*-, -*rat*-, and -*cat*-.

ABC adjectives
Ages: 7 and older.
Number of players: 2 or more.
Place: Indoors or outdoors.

The first player makes up a sentence that contains one adjective that begins with the letter 'A.' The next player, and each following player in turn, must substitute an appropriate adjective that begins with the following letter of the alphabet.

Example: The first player says: 'This is an *a*wful car.' The second player says: 'It is a *b*attered car.' The third player says: 'It is a *c*rashed car.' The fourth player says: 'It is a *d*isgusting car,' and so on.

Any player who cannot continue the game by naming an appropriate adjective at his turn, drops out of the game for that round. Once 2 players have dropped out of the game, they start their own game among themselves, including others as they drop out. The game continues until all but a single player have dropped out of the first game. He is that game's winner and joins the second group, and so on.

Variation: The first player states a simple declarative sentence that does not include any adjective. The noun of that sentence must begin with the letter 'A.' The second player then repeats this same sentence and adds a phrase, including a noun that begins with the letter 'B,' and so on. *Example:* The first player says: 'I have an *a*pple.' The second player says: 'I have an apple in a *b*asket.' The third player says: 'I have an apple in a basket for the *c*ook,' and so on, right through the alphabet. All other rules remain as in the first game.

In any alphabet game involving younger age groups it is wise to exclude the letters from 'U' to 'Z.' Allow children to use a dictionary or an encyclopedia to look up words and to enlarge their vocabularies, even while they are playing the game.

Silly Willy
Ages: 7 and older.
Number of players: 2 or more.
Place: Indoors or outdoors.

Any one version of this game can only be played once. But different versions can be improvised for succeeding rounds.

The first player, and one who is familiar with the game and with the principle involved, asks the second: 'Silly Willy likes butter, but he doesn't like milk. What does Silly Willy like?'

If the second player fails to be able to tell what Silly Willy likes, the first asks the third: 'Silly Willy likes boots, but he doesn't like shoes. What does Silly Willy like?' The game continues in this manner. Players who answer the first player with a sentence employing different nouns that describe what Silly Willy likes correctly, drop out of the game for that series of turns. The last player to be unable to guess what Silly Willy likes is the loser. In this instance Silly Willy likes anything that contains a double letter.

Other versions of this same game can deal with particular letters or qualities. *Example:* 'Silly Willy likes peas, but he doesn't like sugar.' He only likes things that start with the letter 'P.' 'Silly Willy likes airplanes, but he doesn't like sleds.' He only likes things that have wheels, and so on.

Word associations
Ages: 8 and older.
Number of players: 2 or more.
Place: Indoors or outdoors.

The first player names any noun. The second player must answer with another with which the first can be associated. *Example:* The first player says 'Lion.' The second player says 'Meat.' But if the second player gives a less obvious answer, any player may challenge him to defend it. *Example:* If, in the above cited instance, the second player says 'Fish,' he may, but need not, be challenged. If he answers that a lion keeper did not know that lions don't eat fish, and that he therefore threw one into the lion's cage, he may be considered to have defended his association successfully. A successful challenger gains and an unsuccessful defender loses 2 points. If a response goes unchallenged, or if a challenge is defended successfully, the challenger loses and the second player gains 2 points. The second player then names a different noun for the next, and the game continues as at first.

An adult referee should arbitrate all disputes arising from

this game among younger players. But when played by older age groups, the admissibility of a challenged player's defence may be decided by a majority vote among all players. Encourage discussion and give wide latitude to players who defend their associations.

Vocabulary

Ages: 8 and older.
Number of players: 2 or more.
Equipment: Thesaurus.
Place: Indoors.

The first player names an adjective. The second player must then name as many words as he can think of that mean more or less the same thing. *Example:* The first player says 'Big.' The second player says 'Large, great, huge, immense, enormous, vast, monstrous,' and so on. The second player scores according to the number of admissible words that he has named. Any player may challenge him. The Thesaurus decides admissibility of any word. At the end of each turn, that player names another adjective for the next player, and play continues as at first.

When challenged successfully, a player loses 2 points and the challenger gains 5 points. If the challenge is unsuccessful, the challenger loses 5 points and the player gains 5 points. That player wins who has the highest score when all players have had an equal number of turns in successive rounds.

Scrambled letters

Ages: 8 and older.
Number of players: 2 or more.
Equipment: 26 (or more) small squares or slips of paper, about 2·5 × 2·5 cm (1 × 1 inch) each. Write one letter of the alphabet on each. Prepare several sets for older age groups.
Place: Indoors.

All letters are shuffled and turned face down in the centre of the table. The first player, chosen by lot, takes three slips of paper from the centre and turns them face up. If possible, he makes a word out of two or more of the letters. Each following player then continues and plays in the same manner as the first, until all have had one turn. Thereafter, each player continues to draw one letter in turn, using it for different words in combination with other letters or words he already has placed in front of himself on the table.

At his turn, each player may demand from any other player either whole words or individual letters that another has in front of him on the table, which he can use to enlarge a word he has already placed or to make a new word, using one or more of his own letters. That player wins who, after all letters in the centre have been drawn, has used the largest number of letters for completed words, placed on the table in front of himself, after he has deducted all unused letters that he drew and was not able to use to make words. A player, in his turn, may not demand individual letters that form part of a completed word from another player.

Challenges may be made and scored as in the previous game (see Vocabulary).

Blackboard relay
Ages: 8 and older.
Number of players: Two teams of 6 or more players each.
Equipment: Schoolroom blackboard and chalk (or large sheet of wrapping paper, tacked to a wall, and 1 black felt-pen or crayon, if game is played in a room other than a classroom) for each team.
Place: Indoors.

Players are divided into two teams. A line is drawn down the middle of the blackboard. Or, if played not in a schoolroom, two sheets of large wrapping paper should be hung at shoulder height at an equal distance from both teams; one for each.

All players sit down. Each team decides on an order in

which players are to run. At the command from the teacher or referee, the first member of each team races to the blackboard (or paper), picks up the chalk (or felt-pen), and writes the first word of a sentence that he thinks of on the blackboard or paper. He then runs back to his own team and hands the chalk or pen to the next player, who writes a second word next to the first, and so on.

That team wins whose last player is first to return to his seat or place among his teammates, provided his team has completed a full sentence and that all words are spelled correctly. If a team ends with an incomplete sentence, the first team member may run again, and so on, until that sentence is complete. Succeeding runners may correct the mistakes of any previous teammate while they are at the blackboard.

Collage
Ages: 8 and older.
Number of players: 1 or more.
Equipment: Newspapers, blunt scissors, paste, and notepaper for each player.
Place: Indoors.

Each player cuts out words and sentences from his newspaper pages and combines them to make up his own story. In a game of several players, a theme may be decided on beforehand, or each player may make up whatever story occurs to him as he goes along, depending on what he finds.

Headword
Ages: 8 and older.
Number of players: 2 or more.
Equipment: 1 blackboard; pencil and paper for each player.
Place: Indoors or outdoors.

The teacher, or the first player, chosen by lot, writes any word on the blackboard. All players, including the one who writes the word on the blackboard, then try to make as many other words as they can think of out of the letters that make up the Headword. Players do not need to use all or any given number of the letters of the Headword, but they are limited to those that appear. They cannot use any letter in a new word they make more often than it appears in the Headword. That player wins who is able to find the largest number of words he can make.

Sample headword

Bridge. Some words that can be made: **Bed, Beg, Bid, Big, Bird, Bred, Die, Dig, Dire, Dirge, Erg, Gird, Grid, Id, Ire, Red, Rid, Ride, Ridge, Rig, Rib.**

This is an excellent game for building vocabulary. Players should be encouraged to look up in a dictionary any words they can't define. Such words should be discussed at the end of each round. Each round may be played for a given time period agreed to before the start of the game.

Missing letters

Ages: 8 and older.
Number of players: 3 or more.
Equipment: Blackboard and chalk (or large piece of paper); pencils (or pens) for each player.
Place: Indoors or outdoors.

The teacher or a player writes the first and last letter of a 4- or 5- (or more) letter word on a blackboard or large piece of paper. He marks an 'x' between the first and last letter of the word for each of the missing letters – e.g., *B x x d* for *Bird*. The rest of the players in turn must try to guess the missing letters. The player who guesses the word writes a new word in the same manner for all others to guess. It is important to limit the game to words of a specified number of letters, or to establish a minimum and maximum number of letters, depending on the ages and abilities of the players.

Variation: Each player is given his own piece of paper and pencil and writes his own name on it. Below his name he writes the first and last letter of a noun as before, and then passes the paper to the next player to his right. Each player who correctly guesses the word given him scores 10 points. The winner is the player who has the highest score at the end of a given number of rounds.

Buried words
Ages: 8 and older.
Number of players: 3 or more.
Equipment: Blackboard and chalk (or paper and pencil for each player).
Place: Indoors or outdoors.

Each player in turn writes down a sentence in which a noun (name of a city, country, animal, person, fruit, or any other) is buried, because portions of the noun are split up between several words that mean something else entirely.
Examples:
I ama**ze Bra**zilians with tricks.
Jane **came l**ast.
Carpenter**s nail** boards.
    Each player passes his paper to the next and tries to find the buried word in the sentence that is passed to him in turn.
Variation: The teacher, or the first player chosen by lot, composes one sentence, like those described and shown above, and writes it on the blackboard. The first player to guess the hidden word may then make up a new sentence to be written on the blackboard and guessed by the rest, and so on.

Anagrams
Ages: 8 and older.
Number of players: 2 or more.
Equipment: Paper and pencil for each player.
Place: Indoors or outdoors.

Each player is required to think of a 5-letter noun (limited, if desired, to animals, place names, or any other category). He then writes down the letters of the word so that they are totally scrambled, and passes his jumbled word to the next player to his right. The player wins who first unscrambles the letters and forms either the original word or any other word, using all the letters given him by his neighbour to the left. Of course, words of more than 5 letters may be used if the players so decide in advance.

Variation: Before he passes his paper to the next player, each player scrambles a list of 3 or more nouns, or a short sentence of 5 words in which each word, though scrambled, is written separately.

Earth, water, or air
Ages: 8 and older.
Number of players: 2 or more.
Place: Indoors or outdoors.

Players sit in a circle or decide on a sequence in which play passes from one to the next. The first player, chosen by lot, calls out either 'Earth,' 'Water,' or 'Air.' The next player in turn must name an animal that lives in whichever element is named. If he fails to do so, he loses his turn and 1 point. If he names an appropriate animal, he then has the right to name one of the elements for the next player, and so on. This game continues until one player has lost 10 points, or for a pre-determined time period. The player with the lowest score is the winner.

Letter ladder
Ages: 9 and older.
Number of players: 2 to 4.
Place: Indoors or outdoors.

The first player thinks of any word and names its first letter only – e.g., 'P' for pump. The second player thinks of any word beginning with the named letter and names its second letter – e.g., 'A' for pancake. Play continues thus in turn until any player completes a word to which a following player cannot add another letter to change it or to make it longer. A player who at his turn fails to do so scores 1 point and begins another word as at first. That player wins, after each has had the same number of turns, who has the lowest score.

It is best to keep the number of players small, especially with younger age groups. If many players wish to play the same game, divide them into groups of three or four, each group playing the game among its own members.

Variation: All the same rules apply, except that specific categories are agreed to before the start of the game, e.g., foods, furniture, vehicles, boys' or girls' names.

Puzzle word
Ages: 9 and older.
Number of players: 2 or more.
Equipment: Pencil and sheet of paper for each player.
Place: Indoors.

Each player draws a 7·5 cm (3 inch) square on his own sheet of paper and divides it into 9 smaller squares (see diagram). He then decides on a 9-letter word and writes that word into his square, 1 letter per space. The letters must be arranged so that, starting with the first, each following letter is placed into an adjacent square that has a common side with the previous one.

The example, using the word 'elephants,' shown here, demonstrates one way in which the letters must be written down so that, starting with the letter 'E' a pencil line can connect all the letters in their proper order, going from one square to the next, without doubling back across any square or letter.

Once every player has made his own puzzle out of sight of all others, each passes his paper to the next player to his right, who then tries to solve it. That player wins who solves his puzzle first.

Mosaic
Ages: 9 and older.
Number of players: 3 or more.
Equipment: Blackboard and chalk; 2 pieces of paper and 1 pencil for each player.
Place: Indoors.

Each player in turn writes any noun he chooses on the blackboard or on a large sheet of paper that all can see. All players are then required to write a story, using all the nouns listed. Each may use the nouns in any order he chooses.

The memory game
Ages: 9 and older.
Number of players: 8 or more.
Place: Indoors or outdoors.

Players sit in a circle or decide on the order of play. The first player, chosen by lot, declares what he has for sale. *Example:* 'I sell apples.' The next player, and each in turn, also declares what he has for sale. After all players have declared themselves, the first player announces: 'My neighbour has . . . for sale,' naming whatever the second player declared previously. Each player continues to announce his next neighbour's goods until all have spoken. Any player who fails to remember what his neighbour has for sale is out of the game.

At the end of that round, the first player announces what the next two players have for sale, and so on. The object is to see who can remember, in subsequent rounds, the goods first declared for sale by each, for an increasingly large number of players. The problem is made more difficult when players drop out of the game. But if each player pays attention, he is reminded by the players who follow him in the present round of what remains for sale in the next one.

Variation 1: One player is chosen as first speaker. He says: 'I live in a city.' The next player must repeat that sentence and add one of his own. *Example:* 'I live in a city. In that city there is a street.' Each player thereafter in turn must repeat all previously spoken sentences and add one of his own that is related and makes sense.

Any player who fails to repeat the previous part of the story is out of the game. The story goes around until all but one player are out. He is the winner.

Variation 2: Once players have caught on to the principle of this game, they can begin each new round with any sentence of the first player's choice.

Cablegram
Ages: 9 and older.
Number of players: 2 or more.
Equipment: Pencil and paper for each player.
Place: Indoors.

Each player in turn calls out one letter (or more if less than 3 players are in the game) of the alphabet. Each writes down every letter as it is named. The object is for each player to compose a cable message, using the letters in the given order as the first letters for each succeeding word. The messages must make sense.

Example:
W P F B W I Y C H S
Will Pay For Broken Window If You Come Home Soon

or

Willy Please Forgive Betty Where Is Your Cousin Henry Staying

Variation: The first player, chosen by lot, and every other player in successive rounds, gives his first or last name. The letters that make up this name then become the initials for each of the words to be used for the Cablegram.

Hangman

Ages: 9 and older.
Number of players: 2 or more.
Equipment: Blackboard (or pencils and paper for each player).
Place: Indoors.

The teacher, or a player chosen by lot, decides on a long word, or the first line of a nursery rhyme, or other short sentence that is well known to all players. He then draws a series of dots on the blackboard or paper, each representing one letter of the word or sentence, with each group of dots representing one word separated from the next. *Example:* 'I am silly,' would be shown as:

●   ● ●   ● ● ● ● ●

Each player in turn may then guess any letter of the alphabet. When he guesses a letter that is part of the sentence and that has not yet been entered, then the first player or teacher must write it in over the proper dot. In case of a double-letter word, or whenever the same letter appears more than once in a sentence, the first player has the choice of placing a properly guessed letter wherever it fits. But the second identical letter is not put down until another player guesses it again.

If a player fails to guess a letter that can be written over a dot, he draws a circle for the first error, a line each for the body, legs, and arms of a stick man for each of the following errors, one line of a gallows for each of the following errors, a rope and finally a noose around the stick man's head for the rest, one line for each error (see illustration). When a player

completes his drawing, he is out of the game. The player wins who either names the last remaining open letter or who guesses the whole sentence even before all the letters are named. Any player who tries to guess the whole sentence, but fails, must add two strokes to his hanged man at that turn.

Geography
Ages: 9 and older.
Number of players: 2 or more.
Place: Indoors or outdoors.

The first player names a city, county, or country. The next player must name another one of these that begins with the same letter as the last letter of that named by the first player. Each following player continues, and so on, always using the last letter of the city, county, or country named by the preceding player as the first letter for that which he names. Any player who is unable to name another city, county, or country according to these rules, is out of the game. That player wins who is the last remaining in the game.
Example:
First player: London; Second player: Nottingham; Third player: Munich . . . and so on.
Variation: The same game can be played with less experienced players, using animal names.

Alphabet travels
Ages: 9 and older.
Number of players: 3 or more.

Place: Indoors or outdoors.

Each player in turn, starting with the first, who is chosen by lot, must make up a sentence, the principal words (nouns, adjectives, and verbs) of which begin with the letter of the alphabet that applies to his turn. The first player uses all 'A's,' the second all 'B's,' and so on. Each player must start with 'I am going to . . .' and then name a place that begins with the letter to be used at his turn. The letter 'X' is eliminated.

Example:

First player: 'I am going to Africa, to ask an Ashanti for apricots.'

Second player: 'I am going to Boston to buy baked beans.'

Third player: 'I am going to California to collect cheap crops.'

Fourth player: 'I am going to Denmark to dunk delicious doughnuts.'

A player is out of the game if he fails to construct the suitable sentence within the time allowed by common agreement before the start of the game. The last remaining player is the winner.

Variation 1: When the game is played in school, the players may be asked to write their sentences on a blackboard in turn. Or each may be required to write out, on his own sheet of paper, 22 such sentences (eliminating 'V,' 'X,' 'Y,' 'Z'), using the letters of the alphabet. The player who first completes all 22 sentences is the winner. Or each player may be required to begin his sentence with 'In my Zoo, I have a . . .' The name of each mammal, fish, or any other animal must begin with the first, second, and so on letter of the alphabet in turn. Any number of other variations can be improvised, depending on the players' ages, knowledge, or the information to be dramatized.

Variation 2: For ages 12 and above. Each player is given paper and pencil or pen and required to write, within a given time period, a short story of 50 (or more, or less) words, in which each noun, adjective, and verb must begin with a letter of the alphabet specially assigned to him. Anyone who fails to complete his story is out of the game. Those players who complete their stories at the end of the agreed-to time period, read them aloud to the rest.

Twenty questions

Ages: 9 and older.
Number of players: 2 or more.
Place: Indoors or outdoors.

One player is chosen by lot to be 'it.' He decides, silently to himself, on any object, person, animal, or plant. Having made his decision, he provides a clue to the rest of the players by announcing whether it is *animal, vegetable,* or *mineral.* It must be one of these, but may not be a combination of two or more. For example, a 'car' is made of materials that belong to at least two of the three; e.g., rubber tyres (vegetable) and a metal frame, body, and engine (mineral).

Each other player in his turn may then ask a single question that must be answerable by 'it' with either Yes or No. If the others are unable to guess what 'it' thought of by the twentieth question, he wins and thinks of another object, person, animal, or plant, and the game continues as before. If any player guesses what 'it' is thinking of by or before the twentieth question, 'it' has lost and the player who guessed the answer becomes 'it' in turn.

Players who are new to the game should be told to ask the most general questions first, in order to reduce the number of possibilities by a process of elimination. For example, if the clue is 'animal,' the first question might be: 'Is it human?' If the answer is No, the next question might be: 'Does it live on land?' If the answer is Yes, the next question might be: 'Is it a domestic animal?' . . . and so on.

Variation 1: A form of Twenty Questions in which each

player in turn asks one question of the 'it' player, trying to find out his occupation. 'It' decides on a profession before the start of the game. He gives players no clues whatsoever. All other rules remain the same. If players are familiar with different classifications of work, 'it' may be required to state whether he is in a profession, trade, service, or craft, before the start of the game.

Variation 2: For older children, combinations of categories may be allowed, and a fourth category, *abstract*, may be added.

Boutes-rimes (Rhymed ends)

Ages: 10 and older.
Number of players: 3 or more.
Equipment: Blackboard and chalk (or paper and pencil for each player).
Place: Indoors or outdoors.

This game was first played in France in 1648, and invented by the poet Dulos. It became fashionable across all of Europe, and a favourite parlour game among adults.

Each player in turn writes down 4 words on the right-hand margin of his paper. The first and third, and the second and fourth words must rhyme.

Example:

If you were a **fish**   you'd make a good **dish**
that swam in the **sea**   and dinner for **me.**

Each player passes his paper to the next player to his right, who is then required to add a phrase so that each line ends with the given word to form a poem (see example above). Each round is played for a time period agreed to before the start of the game. Only completed poems score, each line counting 10 points for the player who wrote it. That player wins who scores the greatest number of points during a given number of rounds.

Variation: The teacher, or a player chosen by lot, writes the 4 words on a blackboard. All other players are required to compose a poem, as above, using the same words. All poems are read aloud at the end of a given time period. Players vote for the best poem after each round.

Doublets

Ages: 10 and older.
Number of players: 1 or more.
Equipment: Paper and pencil for each player (or blackboard and chalk).
Place: Indoors or outdoors.

Players agree on 2 words, each having the same number of letters. The object of each player is to transform the first word into the second by changing one letter in succeeding step words, until the letters spell the agreed-upon second word. Each new step word must be a real word. The player who reaches the second word in the fewest steps is the winner.

Example: How to change *head* into *feet*:

Head		
Heed	=2 steps	
Feed		
Feet		

Note the changed letter in each step. Other typical transformations include how to change *rain* into *hail*, *boy* into *man*, *hand* into *legs*, *bite* into *nuts*, *flour* into *bread*. It is done as follows, in the least possible number of steps.

rain	boy	hand	bite	flour
into	into	into	into	into
hail	man	legs	nuts	bread
Rain	**Boy**	**Hand**	**Bite**	**Flour**
Rail	Bay	Land	Site	Floor
Hail	May	Lend	Sits	Flood
	Man	Lens	Sets	Blood
		Legs	Nets	Brood
			Nuts	Broad
				Bread

Writing a novel
Ages: 10 and older.
Number of players: 2 or more.
Equipment: 1 large sheet of paper and 1 pencil.
Place: Indoors or outdoors.

The first player, chosen by lot, writes a short, one-line sentence at the top of the paper. He then folds the paper over once, so that what he wrote is not visible to the next player. The next player writes down a second sentence, folds the paper over as before, and passes it to the next player, and so on. When every player has written his sentence, or when each player has completed the agreed-to number of turns, the paper is unfolded and the sentences read aloud by one player, as if the whole were one continuous story.

The story can be made to seem more continuous if every player after the first is required to begin his sentence with: 'And then . . .'; 'After that . . .'; 'Next . . .'; or 'When . . .'

7
Number Games

Coincidence is the mother of superstition. Many coincidences may occur when numbers are arranged in different ways. And for this reason, among others, people in the past have often attributed magic qualities to numbers. These superstitions were in part encouraged and sometimes firmly believed by the priesthood of early cultures. They were the official keepers of accounts and of the calendar, and were the surveyors of the land. They advanced number skills, kept them to themselves, and endowed them with ritual and mystical magic. The rest of the population regarded numbers with awe.

These early misconceptions about operations with numbers are with us still. They are treated in schools and in classrooms as rituals, rather than as symbols of language. Play with numbers desanctifies them, takes away the dread with which many children regard them, and brings them into the arena of use and usefulness.

Number concepts are a part of language. The ideas of far and near, tall and short, many, few, and none at all are less exact words than the same ideas expressed in numbers. Besides, the possible combinations of letters that make up vocabulary are really much more varied and complex than almost any everyday number operation. For example, the 24 letters of the alphabet most frequently used can be combined in 620,448,-401,733,239,439,360,000 (six trillion trillion) ways. If possible word combinations are added, even within rules of grammar and syntax, the number of possible variations becomes staggering. Despite their comparative simplicity and economy, numbers give most children more trouble than words do.

Most mathematical pastimes of the past and present are exercises of logic, skill, or speed. It seems almost as if the use of numbers in play was still considered a solitary pastime, a reminder that in some former age such activities were looked upon as heretical when exercised by any member of the tribe other than those officially appointed by custom and by law.

There are countless solitaire number puzzles and paradoxes. These do not concern us here. Some, like Zeno's puzzle, are insoluble. He suggested, and proved logically, that if you continue to halve the distance between two points, A B, starting from A, you'll never arrive at B. Theoretically, he was right of course. A recognition of the contradictions between everyday experience and symbology can teach students valuable lessons. It can make them aware that numbers, like letters, are an imperfect means of communication, and that unless they are expressed in terms of human need and experience, they can be meaningless and even misleading.

The number games I have adapted, with one or two exceptions, do not go back as far in history as most other games. They are far fewer in number than any other category of games, probably for all the reasons given above.

But all games have a mathematical basis. Any strategy can be calculated in advance and expressed numerically or algebraically, including chance, when the number of possible moves, players, and other given factors are known. Even the winning strategy for games like tic-tac-toe can be stated in mathematical terms.

I have left out of this text any of the formulae or the explanations of mathematical principles on which these games are based. Instead, I hope that players will be encouraged to discover some of the patterns themselves through manipulation of numbers in play. As in all learning, pattern recognition is the dawning of understanding. Using objects and symbols as sets, and viewing mathematical operations as language tools, should help to free children from considering the quantification of qualities and events a dull schoolroom chore.

Odds and evens
Ages: 5 and older.
Number of players: 2 or more.
Equipment: Small pebbles (or coins or beans).
Place: Indoors or outdoors.

The first player chosen by lot to be 'it' holds the pebbles in his hands behind his back, counting out whatever number he chooses into his right hand. Next he holds both hands out in front of him. Each of the other players in turn must guess whether the number of pebbles in his right hand is an 'odd' or an 'even' number. When all players have made their guesses, 'it' announces whether the number of pebbles in his right hand is odd or even. The pebbles in the 'it' player's right hand are then counted, and if 'it' identified that number correctly, each player is scored a 'winner' or 'loser' accordingly. That player who guesses correctly three times on succeeding turns changes places with 'it.' If 'it' identifies the number he holds in his right hand incorrectly, he changes places at once with the player who first called the right answer at that turn. All players start without score whenever a new 'it' takes his place.

How many fingers?
Ages: 6 and older.

Number of players: 3 or more.
Place: Indoors or outdoors.

Egyptians of 4,000 years ago played this game. It is still known to all children in southern Europe as the game of *Morra*. And in England, children shout, 'Buck, buck, how many horns do I hold up?' as they play this game.

The first 'it' is chosen by lot. All others face away from him. 'It' holds up as many fingers of one hand (or of both hands) as he chooses. The rest must guess the number of fingers he holds up. As soon as each player has made his guess, he turns around and faces 'it.' But he may not give any clue to others who have yet to guess. The first player to guess the right number becomes 'it.' The game continues as at first.

Variation: One player is selected as referee. All the others, on command, hold up as many fingers of one hand as they wish, and at the same time shout out what they believe is the sum of the fingers held up by all players at that turn. Anyone who guesses the right number scores 1 point. Each player keeps his own score with his free hand. As soon as one player receives 5 points, that round ends and the winner becomes the referee. The game continues as before.

Dot tic-tac-toe
Ages: 6 and older.
Number of players: 2 or more.
Equipment: Blackboard and chalk (or paper and pencil).
Place: Indoors or outdoors.

Ten (or 20, or any number that is a multiple of 10) dots are marked on a piece of paper, either at random or arranged in lines. Each player at his turn crosses out one, two, or three dots. A player may cross out the same or any different number of dots at succeeding turns. The player who crosses out the last dot is the winner.

Variation 1: Players may be required to name the number of

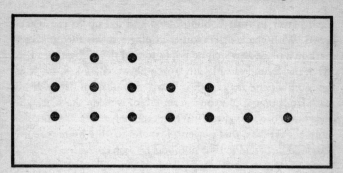

dots they cross out and the sum of the remaining dots at the end of each turn. They should be encouraged to try to calculate their strategies, rather than to cross out dots at random.
Variation 2: Dots are drawn according to the following diagram. If more than two persons play, two lines of dots, each two dots longer than the last, are marked for each additional player. Each player may erase or cross out from one to two dots (no less than one, but no more than two) from any single row at his turn. The loser is the player who, at his turn, must erase or cross out the last dot.

The wheel of fortune

Ages: 6 or older.
Number of players:
2 or more.
Equipment: Draw a large, spoked wheel, 60 cm (24 inches) or larger in diameter, on a blackboard, or on a large sheet of wrapping paper. Write any number in between each spoke of the wheel (see diagram).
Place: Indoors.

Each player in turn is blindfolded and led up to the blackboard. With chalk or crayon each player in his turn makes a mark in a place at which he hopes to find the highest number. If his mark lands inside any space between spokes, he wins that number and may mark it down on a piece of paper. If his mark lands on a spoke, on the rim of, or outside the wheel, he does not score at that turn. When each player has had three or more equal turns, that player wins who has the highest score, provided he has added the numbers he won correctly.

Number guessing
Ages: 7 and older.
Number of players: 2 or more.
Equipment: A heap of pebbles (or marbles, or beans); a jar.
Place: Indoors.

One player is selected as first referee, and fills the jar. Each player in turn tries to guess the number of objects in the jar. They are then counted, and that player who comes closest receives 50 points. Those who lose receive a minus score based on the difference between their guesses and the actual number in the jar. After each turn, the referee or teacher subtracts from or adds to the objects in the jar, and the game continues as before. After a given number of rounds, the player with the highest score wins. He then becomes the referee, and so on.
Variation: This game can also be played with random numbers of dots made on a piece of paper that is passed rapidly from player to player. Each writes down his guess immediately after he has inspected the paper. Each player is allowed only three seconds per turn to inspect the paper.

Odd man wins
Ages: 7 and older.
Number of players: 2.
Equipment: An odd number of pebbles (or counters or marbles) – 15, 17, 19, etc.

Place: Indoors or outdoors.

The counters are heaped or grouped on a table or on the ground. The first player is chosen by lot. Each player may, in turn, draw one, two, or three counters from the pile. After no counters are left in the centre, the player wins who has drawn an odd-numbered sum of counters.

Variation: The same game can be played with an even pile of counters, in which that player wins who has drawn an even sum of counters.

Buzz
Ages: 7 and older.
Number of players: 2 or more.
Place: Indoors or outdoors.

Players sit in a circle. Beginning with the first player, chosen by lot, all players count off by ones – the first player saying 'One,' the second, 'Two,' and so on. The player at whose turn the number 7 is reached, or a multiple of 7 (14, 21, 28, etc.), must say 'Buzz' instead of naming the number. Any player who names 7 or a multiple of 7 is out of the game. The last player to remain in the game is the winner.

Variation 1: On reaching the number 70 (or any of its multiples), the player at whose turn it comes up must say 'Buzz-Buzz.' On reaching 77 (or any multiple), the player must say 'Buzz-Buzz-Buzz.' Any player who fails to do so is out of the game. The rest of the rules remain the same.

Variation 2: Any other number and its multiples may be chosen for the same game. Or, when children are able to manage to keep the number 7 and all its multiples in mind, another number (or any of its multiples) may be added (for example, the number 3), and the player at whose turn it comes up must say 'Fizz.' When a number is reached that is a multiple of both 7 and 3, that player must say 'Buzz-Fizz.'

On the addition of a third number (for example, 5 and its

multiples), the substitute word is 'Quack.' And on addition of a fourth number (for example, 11 and its multiples), the substitute word is 'Cock-a-doodle-doo.' Thus, the player at whose turn 15 comes up is required to say 'Fizz-Quack.' The number 77 becomes 'Buzz-Cock-a-doodle-do,' and 105 becomes 'Buzz-Quack-Fizz.'

Any other numbers may, of course, be substituted, to give the game greater variety in succeeding rounds.

Century game
Ages: 8 and older.
Number of players: 2 or more.
Equipment: Blackboard and chalk (or pencil and paper for all players).
Place: Indoors or outdoors.

The first player, chosen by lot, writes down any number between 1 and 10. Each player in turn adds a similar number and writes the resulting sum. Play continues in turn. That player wins whose final addition brings the sum to exactly 100, but no more. Depending on the number of players, this game requires a good deal of strategy once the sum of the numbers exceeds about 70.

Variation 1: Each player may add a number no greater than 15, 20, or 25, but no less than 10 (or 9 or less). This game can also be played to a winning score greater than 100, depending on the players' ages, by common agreement before the start of the game.

Variation 2: This game may also be played in reverse. Players start with the sum of 100 (or more). Each in turn then subtracts a number no greater than 10 (or whatever number is chosen) and no less than 1. That player wins at whose turn the number 1 is reached.

Variation 3: Any of these games may be played so that a player loses the game if 100 (or more) is reached by addition, or 1 is reached by subtraction, at his turn. All the other rules or their variations remain the same.

Magic squares

Ages: 9 and older.
Number of players: 2 or more.
Equipment: Blackboard and chalk (or pencil and paper for each player).
Place: Indoors or outdoors.

2	7	6
9	5	1
4	3	8

6	1	8
7	5	3
2	9	4

8	1	6
3	5	7
4	9	2

Each player divides a large square into 9 smaller ones (see diagram). Each player is required to place one each of the numbers from 1 to 9 into the squares, so that the sum of any three numbers placed in a straight line (vertically, horizontally, and diagonally) adds up to 15 in every case. The player who first solves this problem is the winner.

Variation 1: Using a similar square, divided into nine equal, smaller ones, and the numbers 1, 2, 3, 10, 11, 12, 19, 20, and 21, each player must place one per square so that any 3 numbers in a straight line in any direction add up to 33.

20	1	12
3	11	19
10	21	2

Variation 2: Each player draws a diagram like that shown overleaf, and places the numbers 1 to 11 into all the circles of

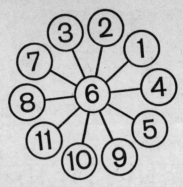

the wheel (see diagram) so that the sum of any three numbers in circles connected in a straight line adds up to the same as all other sets of three circles. That player wins who first solves this puzzle.

Variation 3: Each player places the numbers 1 to 7 into the seven circles shown below (see diagram) so that the sum of the numbers of any three circles connected by lines adds up to 12.

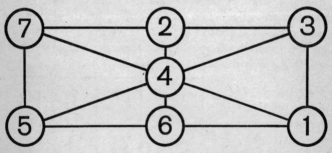

Variation 4: Each player draws and divides a large square into 16 equal smaller ones (see diagram). He then arranges the numbers 1 to 16, one per square, so that the sum of any four squares in each row (horizontal, vertical, and diagonal) adds up to 34.

1	15	14	4
12	6	7	9
8	10	11	5
13	3	2	16

Number tic-tac-toe

Ages: 9 and older.
Number of players: 2.
Equipment: Blackboard and chalk (or pencil and paper).
Place: Indoors or outdoors.

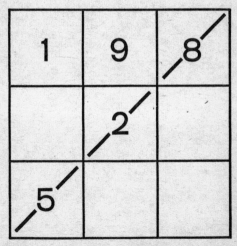

Draw a nine-square tic-tac-toe diagram (see diagram). One
player uses the even numbers between 1 and 10 (2, 4, 6, 8); the

other player uses only the odd numbers (1, 3, 5, 7, 9). The odd-number player has one extra number and goes first, placing one of his numbers into any square. The second player follows in turn, and so on. Each player may use each of his numbers only once. The object is for each player to make a row of three numbers in any direction (vertically, horizontally, or diagonally), the sum of which is 15. That player wins who first succeeds in doing so.

Players change from even to odd numbers in alternate rounds.

8
Party Games

The children of India and Japan enjoy special holidays devoted to them, each with its particular toys, games, and sometimes parties held in their honour. Few cultures cherish children or celebrate childhood in this public a manner. Only Christmas and birthdays remain occasions on which our children are favoured in such a fashion.

This is no coincidence, since we do not treat childhood as an especially worthwhile time of life. As Philippe Ariès[1] points out, Western culture has extended the period of immaturity during the past four hundred years. But at the same time it has certainly treated childhood as a handicapped period, which authoritarian education has simultaneously sought to overcome and managed to prolong. This contradiction may be one cause of the disorientation of many of our young.

I do not suggest that game-playing will solve this problem. But it can allow children to savour some of the exuberance that is their exclusive property and to get a foretaste of independence and self-government. It is one of the few, if often misdirected, privileges we still allow them. A party is a good time to encourage and to stimulate children's games.

Children's parties do not happen. They need planning and supervision. Food and drink, if they are served, and unobtrusive management by adults, are quite as important as treats, decorations, presents, or even games. Adults generally reveal their true concerns about children when they attend and supervise a children's party.

Food. Finger foods are best for any kind of children's party. Hamburgers or frankfurters, potato crisps, raw carrots, and small tomatoes, cake, ice cream, and a fruit punch are probably the most successful menu. It can be prepared beforehand. These foods can be easily served, eaten, and drunk from paper plates and cups. This kind of forethought makes a children's party enjoyable for adults and for children.

Adults. For preschool children, indoor parties at home should be kept small – four to six children at the most. You should have one adult solely concerned with food preparation and serving, plus two others to supervise the children. The ratio of children to adults can be increased at parties for older children who need less supervision. Still, at least one adult should be in attendance at parties for children up to the age of

On the throw of *any other* double: *either* move 1 counter as many spaces as the sum of the score, *or* move 2 counters, each the number of spaces shown on one die, and throw dice again.

5 If a counter lands on a space occupied by the opponent's counter, that player captures the opponent's counter and removes it from the board for the rest of the game.

6 If one player's counter lands on a space occupied by one of his own, he *must*, at that move, continue it to the next unoccupied space on the board.

7 When a player has lost all but 1 counter:

(a) He moves the counter at once – without throwing the dice – to the nearest corner space: A, F, L, M, R, or X. His last counter may occupy *only* these spaces, for the rest of the game.

(b) At each succeeding turn: on the throw of 1 and any number other than 1 or 6, that counter moves to the next of the corner spaces. On the throw of 6 and any number other than 1 or 6, the counter moves 2 corner spaces. On the throw of 1 *and* 6, the counter moves 3 corner spaces. On the throw of *double* 1, the counter moves 2 spaces *and that player throws again*. On the throw of *double* 6, he moves his counter 4 corner spaces *and throws again*. The player who has lost all but 1 counter may throw again if he throws *any* double, even if it is not a double that allows him to move.

(c) The single counter may capture or be captured only on those 6 gates listed above. However, it may not be captured, even at these points, if it is surrounded by the opponent's counters, one on each of the 2 spaces immediately adjacent to the space it occupies.

(d) If both players are reduced to 1 single counter each, Rule 7 applies to both.

8 The player who captures all of his opponent's counters is the winner.

Game 34: Tourne case
Rules:
1 A game for 2 players; 3 counters of a different colour for each; 2 dice.
2 Counters are arranged on the game field as shown (see diagram).
3 One player races the course from A to L, the other from X to M, according to the rules below. That player wins who first reaches his goal with his 3 counters.
4 Each player in turn throws both dice and moves 1 counter only, as many spaces as the sum of both dice, or moves 2 counters, one the number of spaces shown on one die, the other the number of spaces shown on the other die. The sum of the score may *not* be divided in any other way. Doubles score only *half* the sum of the score thrown, and only 1 counter may be moved on the throw of doubles.
5 A player's own counters may not pass each other.
6 If one player's counter lands on a space opposite a space occupied by one of the opponent's counters, the latter is captured and sent off the board. It must be entered again at

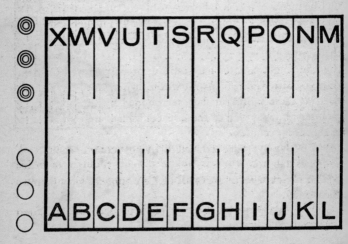

A or X, depending on the side to which it belongs.

7 No more than 1 counter may occupy the same space at one time. If no other move is possible, then that part of the throw at that turn is lost.

Game 35: Six ace

Rules:

1 A game for 2 or 4 players; 12 counters of a different colour for each; 2 dice.

2 If 2 play, 6 counters for each are arranged on the game field as shown (see diagram). If 4 play, counters are arranged as shown. The remaining 6 counters of each player are kept in reserve for use during play.

3 The 6 spaces occupied by each player's 6 counters are his *home*. The 6 counters kept off the field at the beginning of play are the *reserve*. The spaces in the centre of the field (see diagram) are the *pool*.

4 Object of the Game: each player in turn tries to eliminate all of his counters on his home, adding them, according to the

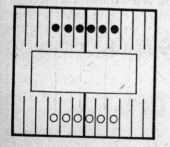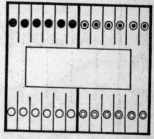

rules, to his opponent's home, his own reserve, or the pool. That player wins who first eliminates all counters from his home, and then is the first to throw a 6 with either of the dice at his turn.

5 Each player throws the dice in turn. Each die is scored separately as follows:

Throw a 1: add 1 counter from your reserve to opponent's home.

Throw a 5: add 1 counter from your reserve to the pool.

Throw a 2: take 1 counter (if any are in the pool) from the pool and add it to your home.

Throw a 6: take 1 counter from your home and add it to your reserve.

Throw a 3 or a 4: no score – no move is made.

Throw double 2: take 2 counters from pool and add them to your home (or up to 2, or none, depending on number of counters in pool).

Throw any other double: move for each die as above, and throw again.

6 In a game of 4 players, all above rules apply. Turns are taken from left to right. Each player adds to or takes from the home of the player on his left at each turn.

Game 36: Fayles

Rules:

1 A game for 2 players; 15 counters each, black for one player, white for the other, or marked so that opponents' counters are easily distinguished; 3 dice.

2 Counters are arranged on the game field as shown (see diagram).

3 The player of the white counters moves *counter-clockwise*, according to the rules. The player of black moves *clockwise*. L is the exit gate for white; M is the exit gate for black (see diagram).

4 Each player at his turn throws the dice and moves any 3 counters. Each counter may move as many gates as the points shown on one of the 3 dice. Or a player may move 1 counter as many gates as the sum of all 3 dice. The score may not be divided in any other way.

5 Each player completes the course indicated in Rule 3. The player wins who first moves all of his counters off the field

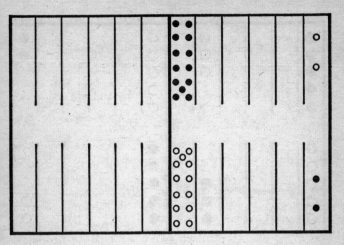

through his exit gate.

6 A counter may not pass or land on a gate occupied by 2 of the opponent's counters.

7 If a counter lands on a gate occupied by 1 of the opponent's counters, the latter is sent off the field and must be entered again at gate L or M, depending on whether it is black or white.

8 If a player at his turn cannot use *all* of his throw of the dice, *he loses the game.*

Game 37: Modern backgammon

Rules:

1 A game for 2 players; 15 counters of a different colour for each; 2 dice.

2 Counters are arranged on the game field as shown (see diagram). Dice are thrown for first move.

3 Each player moves 1 counter per turn as many spaces as points shown uppermost on the dice. A player moves his counters from their starting position in the following direction: from his opponent's inner table to his opponent's outer

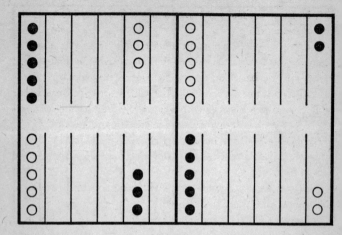

table, to his own outer table, to his own inner table, according to the rules. Each player thus moves in an opposite direction, starting any of his counters from any position at the beginning of the game. That player wins who first bears-off all his counters from his own inner table, according to the rules.

4 *Dice Throws:* counters are moved according to the throw of both dice:

(a) The sum of the points shown on both dice at one turn may be used to move 1 counter as many spaces, *or*

(b) The score of each die may be used to move 2 counters at one turn, each as many spaces as the points shown on one or the other of the dice. The dice score may not be divided in any other way.

(c) On the throw of a *double*, the score is doubled at that turn. One counter can be moved 4 times as many spaces as the points shown on one die, *or* the score may be divided among 2, 3, or 4 counters, moving each as many spaces as shown on 1 die or multiples thereof. The score may not be otherwise divided.

(d) If a player can make use of the points shown on only 1

die, he must use the *higher-scoring* die if possible. He loses the rest of the score.

5 When a counter lands on a blot held by the opponent's counter, the latter is captured, removed from the board, and placed on the bar. The opponent *must* at his next turn enter captured counters on the first space of the other player's inner table. None of a player's counters on the field may be moved until *all* captured counters are again entered in the game.

6 A player's counter may not land on a point held by his opponent. If no other move is possible, he loses that turn or part of the score.

7 Captures are not mandatory. A player may capture with 2 counters at one turn if the dice allow.

8 *Bearing-off*: A player may not bear-off until:

(a) *All* of his counters have entered his own inner table *and*

(b) Any captured counter – even after bearing-off has started – has completed the track and returned to his inner table. Even after all counters are on the player's own inner table, he may not bear-off if his dice score permits a move, bringing any counter or counters closer to the edge of his inner table. More than 1 counter may be borne-off at a turn if the dice score allows.

9 *Victories:* The first player to bear-off all his counters wins the game. Victories are scored as follows:

(a) If the loser has already borne-off 1 or more counters, a *single victory* is scored.

(b) If the loser has not yet borne-off any counter, a *double victory* or *Gammon* is scored.

(c) If the loser has not yet borne-off any counter *and* has one or more captured counters on the bar, a *triple victory* or *Back-gammon* is scored.

Game 38: Puff

Another version of Backgammon, played in England and Germany.

Rules:

1 A game for 2 players; 15 counters of a different colour for each; 2 dice.

2 Both players enter their counters from outside the field at A, according to the throw of the dice at each turn, going in a counterclockwise direction and bearing-off at X (see diagram, p. 249).

3 The player who first bears-off all of his counters at X, according to the rules, is the winner.

4 All counters belonging to one player must be entered before any of that player's counters already on the field may be moved. Captured counters must be re-entered at A before any other move is made.

5 *Dice Score:* The score of each die is used to move each of 2 counters on every turn. The sum of the throw may *not* be used to move 1 counter. The score of the lower-scoring die must be used first at each turn, before the higher-scoring die is used. If the lower-scoring die cannot be used to move any counter, then the whole of that turn is lost.

6 *Doubles:* The points shown uppermost, as well as those *underneath*, each of the 2 dice, are used to move 4 counters (Rule 5 applies here also). After a player has thrown his *first double* in any game, he gets a second throw at each turn at which he throws another double.

7 For blots, points, and captures, Rules 5, 6, and 7 of Game 37 are followed, except that no more than 2 counters may occupy a point.

8 Counters may be borne-off at any time and from any point or blot on the board, whenever the throw of the dice permits, provided that all player's counters are entered on the board at that time.

Game 39: Tric-trac

Though played on a Backgammon board, this is not a race game, but one that is won by scoring points. Points are won by landing on particular spaces on the field and on blots held by the opponent. Each player must be careful to divide his dice score in the most advantageous manner, because if he fails to take advantage of his score, his opponent may lay claim to the points he might have won had he used his score properly. Tric-Trac was invented in France in the sixteenth century, and is the ancestor of numerous variations still popular in many parts of Europe. Players should rule off a score card and have pencils handy before the game begins.

Rules:

1 A game for 2 players; 15 counters of a different colour for each; 2 dice (see diagram, p. 249).

2 One player at his turn, enters his counters at L; the other enters his at M, each moving his counters around the field counterclockwise, according to the throw of the dice, as in Game 37.

3 In this game, no captures are made, and no counters are borne-off. Players continue to move their counters around the field until one player has reached a score of 25.

4 Scoring:

(a) For the player who enters at *L*:

2 points for landing with 2 counters on L

2 points for landing with 2 counters each on A and F

1 point for landing on a blot held by the opponent

(b) For the player who enters at *M*:

2 points for landing with 2 counters on M

2 points for landing with two counters each on S and X

1 point for landing on a blot held by the opponent

5 After a player has thrown the dice at his turn, he first decides *how* and *which* counters to move. He then marks down his point score, if any. Finally, he actually moves his counters. If he has failed to use his dice score to score points, and his opponent is able to see how this might have been done, the opponent may then, *after the counters have been moved,* claim the points that would have been won by that player, had he planned his moves properly. The opponent then adds these points to his own score.

Game 40: Paumecary

The paying of forfeits and fines, and the right to claim favours from the loser, are ancient rights of winners. Here is a four-teenth-century English version of the game of Tabula in which the winner may slap the loser. It is of course permissible to demand other punishment, forfeits, or favours.

Rules:

1 A game for 2 players; 15 counters of a different colour for each; 2 dice.

2 Only half of the Backgammon board is used (see diagram). Players enter their counters at A, going around A, F, S and bearing off at X.

3 Counters are entered and moved on the throw of the dice at each turn (see Game 38, Rules 5 and 6). Blots can be taken and points piled with as many counters of one player as that player chooses. Opposing players may not share a point.

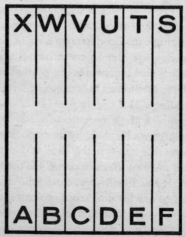

4 When a player has entered *all* his counters, he may then begin to bear-off at X.

(a) When one player has borne-off all his counters, he continues to throw the dice at his turn, to help the losing player enter and move his counters, and to bear them off the board.

(b) For every counter of the opponent borne-off by the winner at his turn, the winner slaps the hand of the loser.

Game 41: Rava

Rules:

1 A game for 2 players; 15 counters of a different colour for each; 2 dice; Backgammon field.

2 All rules for Backgammon apply, in addition to the following:

(a) Each player heaps his 15 counters at A and X respectively at the beginning of the game.

(b) On the throw of a *double*, both top and bottom points of the dice are scored; the move is made, and the dice are thrown again.

(c) Neither player may heap his counters on points on his own side of the board, except on the last space of his own side.

(d) Blots may be taken as in Backgammon, and no counter on a side may be moved until all counters are in play.

(e) Before any counters may be borne off, all of a player's 15 counters must be on the opponent's inner table.

(f) The first player to bear off his counters on the exact throw of the dice wins the game.

Game 42: Emperador

Rules:

1 A game for 2 players; 15 counters of a different colour for each; 3 dice; Backgammon field.

2 Rules 2, 4, 5, and 6 of Game 37 apply, except that:

3 On re-entry of a captured counter, it may not enter if with that score it must land on a point.

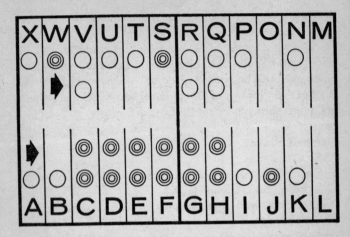

4 Points may be made only on the opponent's side of the board.

5 That player wins who manages to place 2 of his counters on any 6 consecutive spaces on the board (see diagram).

Game 43: Battleships

Rules:

1 A game for 2 players. Each requires one sheet of graph paper (or a sheet of plain paper ruled into $\frac{1}{2}$ cm ($\frac{3}{16}$ inch) squares); one black and one red pencil or magic marker.

2 Both players mark their paper 'A,' 'B,' 'C' . . . along the top edge, starting at the top left hand corner. Then each marks the spaces along the left hand side of the paper '1,' '2,' '3' . . . starting at the bottom left hand corner (see diagram).

3 Each player is allotted the following ships:

1 battleship = 5 squares
1 cruiser = 4 squares
2 destroyers = 3 squares
2 submarines = 1 square each

Every ship is marked by each player on his or her own paper wherever he chooses, out of sight of his opponent. The squares

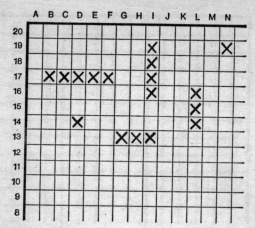

representing each different vessel, other than submarines, must be adjacent in one direction, vertically or horizontally, but never diagonally (see diagram).

4 The first player, chosen by lot, fires one salvo by announcing the coordinates of any square (e.g. '5.D.'). If this square is occupied by a submarine or by any part of any vessel on the opponent's chart, that player must announce a 'hit.' He then places a cross on that square, using his coloured pencil. He does not announce what kind of vessel was hit, unless it was sunk (i.e. a submarine or, in the case of larger vessels, if all squares have been hit in succession). If the square fired on is empty the opponent announces a 'miss.' Play then passes to him and he fires and the game resumes as before. That player wins who first sinks his opponent's entire fleet.

5 Some strategy is involved in playing this game. Players may mark the position of their own salvos in their charts, but neither may move his fleet during the game.

Game 44: Boxes
Rules:

1 A game for 2 or more players. One sheet of plain writing

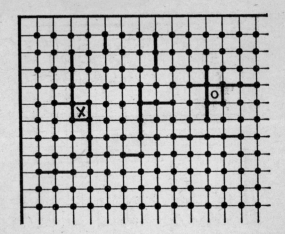

paper; one pencil. If graph paper and one different coloured pencil or felt marker for each player are used, initial preparation and final scoring will be speeded up.

2 Cover the paper with a regular grid of dots, each about ½ cm (3/16 inch) from the next, vertically and horizontally. Or, if graph paper is used, make a fat dot at each intersection of lines (see diagram).

3 Choose order of players by one of the usual methods. The first player, and each player in turn, connects two adjacent dots, up, down or across, but never diagonally, anywhere on the sheet. A player may start from or end at any directly adjacent dot, whether or not it is connected to another. Whenever a player, at his turn, encloses a square, he may then connect two additional dots at that turn. He may continue to connect dots at one and the same turn until the last two dots he connects do not form yet another square (see diagram). On completing a square that player draws his initial inside it.

4 That player wins who has enclosed the largest number of squares when all dots are connected on the sheet.

Age, Place, and
Materials Chart of Games

Note: This chart allows you to find the games and all their variations, listing the lowest age group at which an average child is likely to be able to play and enjoy them; the minimum number of players required to play each game; where each is best played, indoors and out of doors, at home, in school, or in a car; and whether or not special materials, such as a ball, a blackboard, or pencil and paper are required.

Chapter 1 : Ball, bowling, beanbag, and balloon games

Name of game	No of variations	Lowest age	Minimum No players	Indoor Class/home	Gym	Outdoor Hard surface	Soft surface	Page
Pitch ball	1	4	2	X		X	X	33
Bell ball		5	1			X		34
Patsy ball	1	6	1		X	X		35
Sevens		6	1	X	X	X	X	35
Pass the ball	2	6	6		X	X	X	37
Call ball	2	6	5		X	X	X	38
Tag ball	2	6	3		X	X	X	40
Dodge ball	1	6	12	X	X	X	X	40
School ball	7	6	12		X	X	X	41
Catch	3	7	12			X	X	43
Odd ball	1	7	12	X	X		X	44
Throw and go	1	7	5		X	X	X	45
Chase ball		8	4		X	X	X	46
Centre ball		8	10				X	46
Piggyback ball		10	12				X	47
Highball		12	12		X	X	X	48
Bowling games								
Stake ball	1	7	6	X		X	X	52
Ball bowling		7	1	X	X	X		53
Battle ball	1	8	10		X	X	X	54
Ricochet		8	1	X	X	X	X	55

Ball games involving the use of sticks, bats, mallets, and rackets

Game							Page
Trap ball	2	9	2		X	X	59
Hand tennis		12	2	X	X	X	60

Ball games that require marked courts or playing fields

Game							Page
Balloon ball	2	6	12	X	X	X	62
Roll ball		7	6			X	64
Hole ball		7	1			X	65
Relay ball	1	8	24	X	X	X	66
Corner goal ball	1	9	12	X	X	X	67
Rounders	1	9	18		X	X	68

Chapter 2: Marble games

Game							Page
Bounce eye		5	2	X	X	X	76
Marble shoot	5	6	2	X	X	X	77
Target		6	2	X	X	X	78
Ring game		6	2	X	X	X	79
Shoot out		7	2	X	X	X	80
Marble bocce	3	7	2	X	X	X	81
Nine holes		7	2			X	82
Marble bridge	1	7	2	X	X	X	83
Picking the plums	1	7	2	X	X	X	84

Chapter 3: Button games

Game							Page
Button-stringing contest		4	2		X	X	87
Knock 'em down		6	1	X			87
Tiddlywinks	1	6	2	X	X		88
Snap pebble		6	2	X	X	X	89

Name of game	No of variations	Lowest age	Minimum No players	Indoor Class/home	Indoor Gym	Outdoor Hard surface	Outdoor Soft surface	Page
London		7	2	X		X		90
Toss-up		8	2			X	X	91
Chapter 4: Hop, skip, and jump								
Hopscotch	3	5	1			X	X	94
Rope-skipping	7	6	1			X	X	97
Cock-fighting	4	6	2			X	X	100
Leapfrog	1	6	2		X	X	X	100
Hopping bases	4	6	13			X	X	102
Obstacle hop		7	2				X	104
Jump up		7	2			X	X	104
Chapter 5: Race, tag, and catch games								
Running races	2	4	2	X	X	X	X	106
Stoop tag		4	8	X	X	X	X	107
Musical chairs	2	4	8	X				108
Oranges and lemons		4	6	X	X			109
Follow my leader	1	5	6	X	X	X	X	110
Hoop games	2	5	1			X	X	111
Tag	7	5	3			X	X	112
Fox and rabbit		5	10	X		X	X	115
Potato race	1	5	2	X		X	X	115
Pair race		5	13	X		X	X	116
Cat and mouse		5	12		X	X	X	117

Game										Page
Lion and gazelles		6	8	X	X		X	X	X	118
Blind man's buff		6	8	X	X	X	X	X	X	118
Race for the empty space		6	12	X	X		X	X	X	119
Hand-hold tag		6	6	X	X		X	X	X	119
Handkerchief tag		6	10	X	X		X	X	X	120
Counting out catch	1	6	10	X	X		X	X	X	120
Man in the middle	2	6	10	X	X		X	X	X	120
Three's a crowd	2	6	24	X	X		X	X	X	122
Number	1	6	11		X	X		X	X	123
Grandmother's footsteps		6	4	X	X	X	X		X	124
Three legged race		7	4	X	X			X	X	124
Count to one hundred	1	7	6	X				X	X	125
Hand it over		7	24	X	X		X	X	X	125
Relay races	8	7	12	X	X		X	X	X	126
Green and blue		7	12	X	X		X	X	X	128
Slap tag		7	12	X	X		X	X	X	129
Send-off		7	12	X	X		X	X	X	129
Prisoners' base	1	7	10	X	X		X	X	X	130
Poison	2	7	12	X	X		X	X	X	131
About face	1	7	11	X	X	X	X	X	X	132
Indoor tag		7	8		X	X	X			133
Hunt the fox		7	10	X	X		X	X	X	134
Circle-go-round	1	7	12	X	X		X	X	X	135
Wheelbarrow race		7	4	X	X	X	X	X	X	136
Hare and hounds		9	6		X		X	X	X	136

Chapter 6: Word games

Name of game	No of variations	Lowest age	Minimum No players	Use blackboard	Use paper/pencil	Indoors Class/home	In car	Outdoors Camping/beach	Page
Who am I?	1	4	6			X		X	140
Cooperative tale		4	2			X	X	X	141
Nursery rhyme bee		5	2			X	X	X	141
Bird, insect, or fish	3	5	2			X	X	X	142
Because		5	2			X	X	X	143
The ABC game	4	5	2			X	X	X	143
Simon says (O'Grady says)	1	5	3			X	X	X	144
I spy		6	2			X	X		145
All birds fly	1	6	6			X	X	X	145
How many words?		6	6			X		X	146
Eating and drinking game	3	6	2			X	X	X	147
What is my job?	1	6	2			X	X	X	148
Take a trip		7	2	X	X	X			148
Alphabet questions		7	2			X	X		149
Question and answer		7	2			X	X	X	149
Observation	1	7	2		X	X			150
The shopping game	2	7	2			X	X	X	151
Pantomimes	2	7	3			X		X	152
Forbidden words	1	7	2			X		X	154
Definitions		7	2			X	X	X	155

Game									Page
Unfinished story game		7	2				X	X	155
Rumour		7	6			X	X	X	155
Which ant?		7	2			X	X	X	156
ABC adjectives	1	7	2			X	X	X	156
Silly Willy		7	2			X	X	X	157
Word associations		8	2			X	X	X	158
Vocabulary		8	2			X			159
Scrambled letters		8	2		X	X			159
Blackboard relay		8	12		X	X			160
Collage		8	1			X			161
Headword	1	8	2		X	X	X		161
Missing letters	1	8	3		X	X	X		162
Buried words	1	8	3		X	X	X		163
Anagrams	1	8	2	X		X	X		163
Earth, water, or air		8	2			X	X		164
Letter ladder	1	9	2			X	X	X	164
Puzzle word		9	2		X	X	X	X	165
Mosaic		9	3		X	X		X	166
The memory game	2	9	8			X	X		166
Cablegram	1	9	2		X	X	X	X	167
Hangman		9	2		X	X	X		168
Geography	1	9	2			X	X	X	169
Alphabet travels	2	9	3			X	X	X	169
Twenty questions	2	9	2			X	X	X	171
Boutes-rimes	1	10	3	X	X	X	X	X	172

Name of game	No of variations	Lowest age	Minimum No players	Use blackboard	Use paper/pencil	Class/home (Indoors)	In car (Indoors)	Camping/beach (Outdoors)	Page
Doublets		10	1	X	X	X		X	173
Writing a novel		10	2		X	X		X	174
Chapter 7: Number games									
Odds and evens		5	2			X	X	X	177
How many fingers?	1	6	3			X		X	177
Dot tic-tac-toe	2	6	2	X	X	X		X	178
The wheel of fortune		6	2	X	X	X			179
Number guessing	1	7	2			X		X	180
Odd man wins	1	7	2			X		X	180
Buzz	2	7	2			X	X	X	181
Century game	3	8	2	X	X	X		X	182
Magic squares	4	9	2	X	X	X		X	183
Number tic-tac-toe		9	2	X	X	X		X	185
Chapter 8: Party games									
Hunt the thimble	1	4	2			X		X	190
Matching grasses		4	2					X	190
Button, button	2	4	6			X		X	191
Grin or bear it		4	4			X		X	191
Bobbing for apples	1	4	4			X		X	192
Pin the tail on the donkey	1	4	2			X			193
Seek – don't speak		5	4			X			194

Paper-clip fishing		5	2		X	194
Blow-ball	1	5	6		X	195
Soap bubble battle	1	5	2		X	196
Card tossing		5	2		X	196
The swinging game	1	5	2		X	197
Tug of war	2	5	8		X	198
Clothespeg relay		6	8		X	199
Party dots		6	3	X	X	200
Consequences		6	3	X	X	200
Jacks	5	6	2		X	202
Sardines		6	5		X	204
Outlines		6	2	X	X	204
Stone, scissors, and paper		6	2		X	205
Conkers		6	2		X	206
Tangram	1	7	2	X	X	207
Mumbledypeg	1	8	2		X	208

Chapter 9 : Strategic games

Game No	Name	No of players	Page
1	Alquerque	2	217
2	Coyote and chicken	2	218
3	Kono	2	219
4	Warlord	2	220
5	Tiger	2	220
6	Two armies	2	222
7	Cows and leopards	2	222
8	Senat	2	224
9	Block or jump	2	225
10	Derrah	2	226
11	Hasami shogi	2	227
12	Shogi	2	228
13	Draughts	2	228
14	Loser	2	229
15	Diagonal draughts	2	230
16	Dama	2	230
17	French draughts	2	231
18	English draughts	2	232
19	Cops and robbers	2	232
20	Polish draughts	2	232
21	Reversi	2	234
22	Fanorama	2	235
23	Leapfrog	2	236
24	Warriors	2 to 4	237
25	Halma	2 to 4	239
26	By the numbers	2 to 4	240
27	Table	2	241
28	Pachisi (Ludo)	2 to 4	242
29	Three-Men-Morris	2	246
30	Six-Men-Morris	2	246
31	Nine-Men-Morris	2	247
32	Noughts and crosses	2	248
33	Chasing the girls	2	249
34	Tourne case	2	252
35	Six acre	2 to 4	253
36	Fayles	2	254
37	Modern backgammon	2	255
38	Puff	2	257
39	Tric-trac	2	258

Game No	Name	No of players	Page
40	Paumecary	2	260
41	Rava	2	261
42	Emperador	2	261
43	Battleships	2	262
44	Boxes	2 or more	263

Bibliography

1. Ariès, P. *Centuries of Childhood*. New York: Vintage, 1962.
2. Arnold, A. *Teaching Your Child to Learn from Birth to School Age*. Englewood Cliffs: Prentice-Hall, 1971.
3. Arnold, A. *Your Child's Play*. London: Pan Books, 1975.
4. Arnold, A. *The Yes and No Book*. Chicago: Reilly and Lee, 1970.
5. Bancroft, J. H. *Games for the Playground, Home, School and Gymnasium*. New York: Macmillan, 1909.
6. Béart, C. *Jeux et Jouets de L'Ouest Africain*. 2 vols. Dakar: IFAN, 1955.
7. Bell, R. C. *Board and Table Games from Many Civilizations*. London: Oxford University Press, 1960.
8. Caillois, R. *Man, Play and Games*. Glencoe, Ill.: The Free Press, 1961.
9. Champlin, J. D., and Bostwick, A. E. *The Young Folks' Cyclopedia of Games and Sports*. New York: Henry Holt and Co., 1899.
10. Coudeyre, M., and Mathieu, G. A. *Paris Review*. Paris: U.S. Lines, 1956.
11. Culin, S. *Games of the Orient*. Tokyo: Charles Tuttle Co., 1958 (orig. ed., 1895).
12. D'Allemagne, H. R. *Histoire des Jouets*. Paris: Hachette, ca. 1902.
13. D'Allemagne, H. R. *Récréations et Passe-Temps*. Paris: Hachette, ca. 1903.
14. D'Allemagne, H. R. *Sports et Jeux D'Adresse*. Paris: Hachette, ca. 1904.
15. Evans, P. *Hopscotch*. San Francisco: The Porpoise Bookshop, 1955.
16. *Every Boy's Book*. London: George Routledge and Co., 1860.
17. *Every Little Boy's Book*. London: George Routledge and Co., ca. 1880.
18. Falkener, E. *Games, Ancient and Oriental and How to Play Them*. New York: Dover, 1961 (orig. ed., 1892).

19. Furness, J. C. *String Figures and How to Make Them*. New York: Dover, 1962 (orig. ed., 1906).

20. Goldstein, K. S. 'Strategy in Counting Out, an ethnographic folklore field study.' Toronto: American Folklore Society, 1967 (unpublished).

21. Gomme, A. B. *The Traditional Games of England, Scotland and Ireland*. 2 vols. New York: Dover, 1964 (orig. ed., 1894 and 1898).

22. Haddon, K. *Cat's Cradles from Many Lands*. London: Longman's Green and Co., 1911.

23. Huizinga, J. *Homo Ludens*. Boston: Beacon Press, 1955.

24. Leslie, Miss. *American Girl's Book*. Boston: Munroe and Francis, 1851.

25. Loyd, S. *Cyclopedia of Puzzles*. New York: Franklin Bigelow Corp., 1914.

26. Murray, H. J. R. *A History of Board Games*. London: Oxford, 1952.

27. Newell, W. W. *Games and Songs of American Children*. New York: Dover, 1963 (orig. ed., 1883).

28. Opie, I., and Opie, P. *Children's Games in Street and Playground*. New York: Oxford, 1969.

29. Pick, J. B. *The Phoenix Dictionary of Games*. London: J. M. Dent, 1963.

30. *Simulation Games for the Social Studies Classroom*. New Dimensions, Foreign Policy Association, 1969, 1:1.

31. Smith, C. F. *Games and Game Leadership*. New York: Dodd, Mead, 1932.

32. Strutt, J. *The Sports and Pastimes of the People of England*. Thomas Tegg and Sons, 1801.

33. *The Boy's Treasury of Sports, Pastimes and Recreations*. New York: Austin and Co., 1850.

34. Wagner, H. *Illustriertes Neues Spielbuch*. Leipzig: Otto Spamer, 1886.

Picture Sources

Half title: Sargent, E., *Sargent's Standard First Reader*, Boston: L. Shorey, 1866, p. 20.

Title page: Moulidars, T. de, *Un Million de Jeux et de Plaisirs*, Paris: Librairie Contemporaine, ca. 1880, p. 315.

Contents page: Wagner, H., *Illustriertes Neues Spielbuch*, Leipzig: Otto Spamer, 1886, p. 123.

11. *Social Amusements, or Holidays at Aunt Adela's Cottage*, Boston: William Crosby and Company, 1839.

13. D'Allemagne, H. R., *Sports et Jeux D'Adresse*, Paris: Hachette, ca. 1904, p. 59.

17. *The Boy's Treasury of Sports, Pastimes and Recreations*, New York: Austin and Company, 1850, p. 59.

19. Wood, J. G., *The Boy's Modern Playmate*, London: F. Warne and Company, ca. 1890, p. 14.

20. Dilaye, F., *Les Jeux de la Jeunesse*, Paris: Hachette, 1885, p. 302.

21. Wagner, H., *Illustriertes Neues Spielbuch*, Leipzig: Otto Spamer, 1886, p. 123.

25. *Juvenile Games for the Seasons*, Edinburgh: Oliver and Boyd, 1823, p. 43.

27. Cf. page 13; p. 119.

29. Cf. page 17; p. 40.

30. (top). Champlin, J. D., and Bostwick, A. E., *The Young Folks' Cyclopedia of Games and Sports,* New York: Henry Holt and Company, 1899, p. 51.

30. (bot.). Ibid: p. 25.

33. *Every Boy's Book,* London: Routledge and Company, 1860, p. 36.

48. Cf. page 21; p. 36.

50. (top). Strutt, J., *The Sports and Pastimes of the People of England,* Thomas Tegg and Sons, 1801, p. 267.

50. (mid.). Ibid: p. 271.

50. (bot.). Cf. page 13; p. 279.

51. D'Allemagne, H. R., *Récréations et Passe-Temps,* Paris: Hachette, ca. 1903, p. 63.

52. Cf. page 21; p. 148.

56. Ibid: p. 148.

57. Cf. page 50; p. 105.

58. (top). Cf. page 17; p. 25.

58. (bot.). Cf. page 13; p. 171.

59. (top). Cf. half title; p. 65.

59. (bot.). Cf. page 21; p. 28.

60. *Cassell's Book of Sports and Pastimes,* London: Cassell, Peter, Galpin and Company, ca. 1880, p. 227.

69. Cf. page 50; p. 96.

70. *The Holiday ABC Book,* no publ., ca. 1850.

72. Cf. page 13; p. 315.

73. (top). *Harper's Young People,* New York: Harper and Brothers, 1883, p. 380.

73. (bot.). *The Nursery Magazine,* Boston: L. Shorey, Ill: 18, June 1868, p. 175.

74. Cf. page 25; p. 122.

75. (top). Cf. page 60; p. 244.

75. (bot.). Cf. page 21; p. 149.

76. (top). Cf. page 33; p. 17.

76. (bot.). Cf. page 21; p. 149.

83. Cf. page 60; p. 145.

86. Cf. page 13; p. 140.

87. Cf. page 19; p. 177.

92. Cf. page 25; p. 34.

93. Cf. page 19; p. 15.

97. Cf. page 25; p. 124.

99. Cf. page 21; p. 111.

101. Cf. page 17; p. 65.
105. (top). Cf. page 21; p. 109.
105. (bot.). Cf. page 33; p. 5.
108. (top). Cf. page 13; p. 62.
108. (bot.). Cf. page 17; p. 49.
112. Cf. page 33; p. 28.
113. Cf. page 21; p. 83.
118. Ibid: p. 123.
122. Ibid: p. 41.
138. Cf. page 73 (bot.).; VI, 1869, p. 109.
140. Cf. page 19; p. 189.
175. Cf. page 21; p. 123.
187. Cf. page 73 (bot.); XVIII: 3, p. 81.
188. Cf. page 21; p. 41.
192. Cf. page 50; p. 391.
198. Cf. page 19; p. 14.
202. Cf. page 30; p. 443.
203. (top). Ibid: p. 444.
203. (bot.). Ibid.
205. Cf. page 51; p. 151.
208. Cf. page 21; p. 87.
210. Miss Leslie, *American Girl's Book*, Boston: Monroe and Francis, 1851, p. 142.
276. Ibid: p. 320.
277. Cf. p. 50.
279. Cf. page 25; p. 85.
281. Cf. page 13; p. 43.

Note: All other diagrams and illustrations designed by the author.

Index

ABC adjectives, 156
ABC game, The, 143
About face, 132
Age grouping, 15, 21, 25, 27–8, 94, 212 *see also* Game Chart
Aggressiveness, 11–12, 16, 19, 211
All birds fly, 145
All fish swim, 146
Alphabet games, 143–4, 149, 151–2, 156–7, 167–8, 169, 170, 171, 176
Alphabet questions, 149
Alphabet travels, 169
Alquerque, 212, 217, 228, 235, 237
Anagrams, 163

Backgammon, 248–62
Badminton, 58
Ball bowling, 53
Balloon ball, 62–4
Balloon games, 34, 37–8, 41–4, 47, 62–4
Ball(s), 29–71
  cricket, 65
  fives, 61
  foot, 43, 44, 46–7, 52–6, 66–8
  golf, 33, 60
  inflated, 34, 37, 38, 40, 43, 44, 46–7, 52–6, 66–7
  net, 43, 44, 46–7, 52–6, 66–7
  rubber, 34, 35, 38, 41, 45, 59, 60
  soft, 33, 60

table tennis, 33, 90, 195
tennis, 45, 59, 60, 68
Bandy ball, 57
Barley break *see* Man in the middle
Baseball, 58
Basketball, 29, 48
Bat games, 33, 57–61, 68–71
Battle ball, 32, 54 *see also* Norse common ball
Battleships, 262
Beanbag games, 33, 34, 41, 43, 47
Because, 143
Bell ball, 34
Bird, insect or fish, 142
Birthday party games *see* Party games
Blackboard games, 148, 160–63, 166, 168, 172, 173, 178, 179, 182, 183, 185
Blackboard relay, 160
Blind man's buff, 118
Block or jump, 225
Blow-ball, 195
Board game moves, captures and jumps, 212–16
Board games, 9, 210–64
Bobbing for apples, 192
Bocce, 49 *see also* Marble bocce
Bounce eye, 76
Boutes-rimes, 172
Bowling, 49–56
  alleys, 51

on-the-green, 51
pins, 50, 51–6
Bowls *see* Bowling
Boxes, 263
Bubble-the-justice, 52 *see also* Nine holes
Buck, buck *see* How many fingers?
Buried words, 163
Butterfly hunt, 117
Button, button, 191
Button games, 86–92, 191
Button-stringing contest, 87
Buzz, 181
By the numbers, 240

Cablegram, 167
Call ball, 38
Camp, 32
Card tossing, 196
Car games, 138–74
Carry tag, 113
Cat and mouse, 117
Catch, 43
Cat's cradle, 14, 205
Centre ball, 46
Century game, 182
Chance (in game playing), 176, 212
Charades, 153
Chase ball, 46
Chase the fox, 98
Chasing the girls, 249
Cheating, 24–5
Checkers *see* Draughts
Chess, 62, 210, 228, 241
Choosing sides, 21–4
Choosing team captains, 21–4
Circle-go-round, 135
Classroom games, 18, 26, 33, 41, 61, 108, 138–207 *see also* Game Chart
Clothespeg relay, 199
Club ball, 57

Cock-fighting, 100
Coin tossing, 22
Collage, 161
Common ball *see* Norse common ball
Competitiveness, 16, 17, 19–20, 189
Conkers, 206
Consequences, 200
Cooperative tale, 141
Cops and robbers, 232
Corner goal ball, 67
Counters (board game), 210–14
Counting out, 21–4
Counting out catch, 120
Counting rhymes, 23–4
Count to one hundred, 125
Cows and leopards, 222
Coyote and chicken, 218
Cricket, 18, 58
Croquet, 57
Curling-on-the-ice, 50

Dama, 230
Dames *see* Draughts
De cercar la liebre *see* Coyote and chicken
Definitions, 155
Derrah, 226
Diagonal draughts, 230
Dice, 78, 213
Dodge ball, 40
Dot tic-tac-toe, 178
Doublets, 173
Draughts, 228

Earth, water, or air, 164
Eating and drinking game, The, 147
Egg and spoon race, 107
Egg hopping *see* Obstacle hop
Ekaria Dukaria *see* Hopscotch
El-quirkat *see* Alquerque

Emperador, 261
English draughts, 232
Ethics, 10

Fanorama, 235
Fayles, 254
Finger games, 14, 23, 178, 205
Fives, 61
Five stones *see* Jacks
Folk lore, 14, 30 *see also* Historical
   and literary references; Magic;
   Regional references; Ritual
Follow my leader, 110
Football, 10, 18, 31, 32 *see also*
   Ball(s)
Forbidden words, 154
Forfeits, 19, 213
Fox and rabbit, 115
French draughts, 231

Game of Goose, The Royal, 210
Game rhymes, 23, 24, 109–10,
   139–42
Geography, 169
Go, 210
Goff *see* Golf
Golf, 57
Grandmother's footsteps, 124
Green and blue, 128
Grin or bear it, 191
Gymnasium games, 33, 35–45, 46,
   47, 54–5, 62–4, 66–7, 100, 109–10,
   112–14, 117–18, 119, 120, 121,
   122, 124–32, 134–6, 198 *see also*
   Game Chart

Half-bowl, 51
Halma, 239
Handball, 31, 61 *see also* Ball(s)
Hand-hold tag, 119
Hand it over, 125
Handkerchief tag, 120

Hand-over-hand, 22
Hand tennis, 60
Hangman, 168
Hare and hounds, 136
Hasami shogi, 227
Heads or tails *see* Coin tossing
Headword, 161
Hide-and-seek *see* Count to one
   hundred
Highball, 48
Historical and literary references,
   17, 29–33, 36, 46, 51, 57–8, 61–2,
   72–3, 97, 106, 139, 172, 210–12,
   217, 218–48 *see also* Bibliography;
   Folk lore; Myth; Regional
   references
   Alexander the Great, 31
   al-Rashid, Harun, 31
   Ariès, Philippe, 187
   Augustus, Emperor, 31
   Bradford, William, 46
   British Museum, 30
   Caesar, Julius, 31
   Charles V, King, 31
   Chaucer, Geoffrey, 104
   Culin, Stewart, 205
   Delphic oracle, 139
   Duclos, 172
   Edward III, King, 32
   Edward VI, King, 51
   Elizabeth I, Queen, 104, 245
   Evans, Patricia, 94
   Froebel, Friedrich, 15
   Gomme, Alice, 14
   Henry VII, King, 58
   Henry VIII, King, 51
   Homer, 31
   Howard, Dorothy, 14
   Huizinga, Johan, 14, 211
   James I, King, 9, 32
   Margot, 58
   Massachusetts Institute of

Technology, 8
Medieval games, 31, 49, 57, 111, 152, 211
Mime plays, 152
Naismith, James, 29
Neumann, Johann von, 211
Odyssey, 31
Olympic games, 106
Paiget, Jean, 8
Polo, Marco, 205
Shakespeare, William, 246
Strutt, Joseph, 98
Theodosius, Emperor, 106
Zeno, 176
Hole ball, 65
Home, 94–5
Hoola hoop, 111
Hooliganism, 9
Hoop games, 111
Hopping bases, 102
Hopping games, 93–100, 102–4
Hopscotch, 94
Hot or cold *see* Hunt the thimble
How many fingers?, 177
How many words?, 146
Hunt the fox, 134
Hunt the thimble, 190
Hurdle relay, 127
Hurling, 31

Indoor games, 28, 33, 41, 52–3, 55, 62, 76–81, 83–5, 87–91, 106–8, 110, 115–16, 118, 123, 124, 132–3, 136, 140–74, 177–86, 190–97, 199–202, 204–6, 207–8 *see also* Game Chart
Indoor tag, 133
Infant schoolers, games for, 27 *see also* Primary schoolers; Game Chart
I spy, 145

Jacks, 202
Janken *see* Stone, scissors, and paper
Jousting, 57
Jump up, 104

Kayle-pins *see* Skittles
Kemp, 32
Kettle *see* Skittles
Kicking games, 28, 32, 44, 45–6, 52–3
Kittle-pins *see* Skittles
Knock 'em down, 87
Kono, 219
Kotiyo saha harak *see* Cows and leopards

Lacrosse, 48
Leapfrog (contact), 100
Leapfrog (strategic), 236
Learning games, 16, 17, 39, 138–86
Letter ladder, 164
Lion and gazelles, 118
London, 90
Loser, 229
Ludo *see* Pachisi
Ludus Latrunculus *see* Backgammon

Magic, 175, 235
Magic squares, 183
Man in the middle, 120
Marble bocce, 81
Marble bridge, 83
Marble games, 72–85
Marble shoot, 77
Marelles *see* Hopscotch
Matching grasses, 190
Memory game, The, 166
Merelles, 245
Missing letters, 162
Modern backgammon, 255

Mogol Putt'han *see* Two armies
Monopoly, 248
Morality *see* Cheating; Ethics
Morra *see* How many fingers?
Mosaic, 166
Mumbledypeg, 208
Musical bumps, 109
Musical chairs, 108
Musical games, 14, 108, 109
Myth, 30, 36 *see also* Historical and
 literary references; Regional
 references

Netball, 18 *see also* Ball(s)
Nine holes, 82
Nine-men morris, 247 *see also*
 Merelles
Nine pins *see* Skittles
Norse common ball, 32
Noughts and crosses, 248 *see also*
 Tic-tac-toe
Number, 123
Number games, 123–4, 175–86
Number guessing, 180
Number tic-tac-toe, 185
Nursery rhyme bee, 141
Nursery rhyme games *see* Game
 rhymes

Observation, 150
Obstacle hop, 104
Odd ball, 44
Odd man wins, 180
Odds and evens, 177
O'Grady says *see* Simon says
Oranges and lemons, 109
Outdoor games, 28, 33–49, 52–6,
 59–60, 63–71, 76–85, 88–92,
 94–105, 107–8, 109, 110–22,
 124–33, 134–7, 140–44, 145–50,
 151, 152–8, 161–4, 166, 169, 170,
 171–4, 177–8, 181–6, 190–91,

196–9, 202–3, 205–6, 208–9
 see also Game Chart
Outlines, 204

Pachisi, 62, 242
Pair race, 116
Pall-Mall *see* Croquet
Pantomimes, 152
Paper clip fishing, 194
Paper games, 207–8 *see also* Pencil
 games
Party dots, 200
Party games, 187–209 *see also* Ball,
 Marble, Word and Number
 games; Game Chart
Pass the ball, 37
Pass the message, *see* Rumour
Pass the parcel, 109
Patsy ball, 35
Paumecary, 260
Pencil games, 138, 148, 161–4, 165,
 166–8, 172–4, 178, 182–6,
 200–202, 204 *see also* Game Chart
Picking the plums, 84
Piggyback ball, 47
Piggyback games, 47
Piggy in the middle, 44
Pin the tail on the donkey, 193
Pitch ball, 33
Playgrounds *see* Playing fields
Playing card choice, 23
Playing fields, 10, 14, 15, 28, 61–71,
 106
Playing pieces *see* Counters
Play spaces *see* Playing fields
Poison, 131
Polish draughts, 232
Polo, 57
Pon chochotl *see* Coyote and
 chicken
Potato race, 115
Pre-schoolers, games for, 14, 15,

18, 26–7, 139, 212 *see also* Game
Chart
Primary schoolers, games for, 14,
15, 18, 26–7 *see also* Game Chart
Prisoners' base, 130
Prizes, 20
Puff, 257
Puzzle word, 165

Question and answer, 149

Race for the empty space, 119
Race games, 37–8, 42–3, 66–7, 100,
101, 104, 136–7
Racket games, 22
Rava, 261
Regional references
  Afghan games, 57
  African games, 7, 32, 211, 224,
    225, 226, 235
  Arabian games, 217
  Asian games, 7 *see also* Chinese,
    Indian, Japanese, Korean,
    games
  Australian aborigine games, 211
  Bolivian games, 197
  Cameroon games, 30
  Celtic games *see* Irish games
  Ceylonese games, 222
  Chinese games, 94, 152, 205, 220,
    222
  Cretan games, 245
  Czechoslovakian games, 245
  Egyptian games, 30, 205, 217,
    224, 245, 248
  English games, 7, 10, 14, 30, 51,
    57, 61, 72, 94, 97, 104, 178,
    192–3, 229, 241, 243, 245, 257
  Eskimo games, 211
  European games, 7, 57, 93, 152,
    206, 239, 259
  French games, 58, 94, 172, 229,

    232, 245, 259
  German games, 94, 229, 245, 257
  Greek games, 31, 32, 106, 139,
    202, 245
  Indian games (American), 29, 48,
    197, 211, 217, 218, 237
  Indian games (East), 62, 94, 187,
    243
  Irish games, 31
  Italian games, 49, 178
  Japanese games, 32, 152, 187,
    205, 218, 219, 220, 222, 227
  Korean games, 205, 219
  Malagasy games, 235
  Malaysian games, 220–21
  Nigerian games, 226
  Oriental games, 202, 205, 220
    see also Ceylonese, Chinese,
    Indian, Japanese, Korean
    games
  Persian games, 57
  Roman games, 31, 57, 72, 94,
    245, 248
  Russian games, 94, 229, 245, 248
  Saxon games, 241
  Scandinavian games 94, 241
  Scottish games *see* English games
  South American games, 32, 197,
    217
  Spanish games, 217, 218, 237
  United States games, 7, 8, 10, 32,
    48, 73, 94, 95, 206, 218
  Viking games, 245
Relay ball, 66
Relay races, 66, 113, 116, 126
Reversi, 234
Rhymed ends *see* Boutes-rimes
Ricochet, 55
Ring ball, 57 *see also* Croquet
Ring game, 79
Ritual games, 30, 61, 175, 197, 237
  see also Myth

Role playing, 17–18
Roll ball, 64
Rope skipping, 97
Rounders, 68
Rugger, 31
Rules (general), 8, 9, 10, 16, 17, 18,
  25, 26, 73–5, 94, 139, 212 *see also*
  individual game rules
Rumour, 155
Running games, 106–37

Sack race, 107
Sardines, 204
School ball, 41
Scrambled letters, 159
Seega *see* Senat
Seek – don't speak, 194
Senat, 224
Send-off, 129
Sevens, 35
Shadow tag, 114–15
Shogi, 228
Shoot out, 80
Shopping game, The, 151
Silly Willy, 157
Simon says, 144
Six ace, 253
Six-men morris, 246
Sixteen soldiers *see* Two armies
Skill development, 16, 25–6
Skittles, 51
Slap tag, 129
Snap pebble, 89
Snip-snap *see* Tiddlywinks
Soap bubble battle, 196
Sports, 16, 18, 28 *see also* Baseball,
  Cricket, Football, Lacrosse,
  Netball
Squash, 58
Stake ball, 52
Stone, scissors, and paper, 205
Stool ball, 46

Stoop tag, 107
Stow ball, 57
Strategic games, 62, 210–64 *see also*
  Game Chart
String games, 14, 87
Sukari musachi *see* Coyote and
  chicken
Swinging game, The, 197

Table, 241
Tabula *see* Backgammon
Tag, 112
Tag ball, 40
Tag games, 39, 40–41, 47, 53, 65,
  70, 102, 108, 113–15, 116–24,
  128–36
Take a trip, 148
Tangram, 207
Target, 78
Team captains *see* Choosing—
Teenagers, 15, 18
Television, 7, 10, 13, 15, 16, 31, 93,
  140
Tempelhüpfen *see* Hopscotch
Tennis, 58
Three-legged race, 124
Three-men-morris, 246
Three's a crowd, 122
Throw and go, 45
Tic-tac-toe, 178
Tiddlywinks, 88
Tiger, 220
Tops, 14
Toss-up, 91
Touch tag, 113
Tourne case, 252
Toys, 14, 30, 139
Trap ball, 59
Travel games, *see* Car games
Tric-trac, 258
Tug of war, 198
Twenty questions, 171

Two armies, 222

Unfinished story game, The, 155

Vocabulary, 159

Warlord, 220
Warriors, 237
What is my job ?, 148
Wheelbarrow race, 136

Wheel of fortune, The, 179
Which ant ?, 156
Who am I ?, 140
Word associations, 158
Word games, 138–74
Writing a novel, 174

Yasasukari musachi *see* Coyote and
  chicken